THE MONK AND
THE SLY CHICKPEA

Evthókimos Koskinás, The Monk

THE MONK AND THE SLY CHICKPEA

TRAVELS ON CORFU

THOMAS K. SHOR

City Lion Press Edition

This book was originally
published as Part I of *Windblown Clouds*
Escape Media Publishers, USA 2003

© Thomas K. Shor 2019
All Rights Reserved

ISBN: 9780999291849

CITY LION
PRESS

Left to his own resources, man always begins again in the Greek way—a few goats or sheep, a rude hut, a patch of crops, a clump of olive trees, a running stream, a flute.

Henry Miller

Other Books by Thomas K. Shor:
(see page 126 for details)

Prose:

A STEP AWAY FROM PARADISE:
THE TRUE STORY OF A TIBETAN LAMA'S JOURNEY
TO A LAND OF IMMORTALITY
(Penguin 2011 & City Lion Press 2017)

INTO THE HANDS OF THE UNKNOWN
AN INDIAN SOJOURNE WITH A HARVARD RENUNCIENT
BEING PART II OF *WINDBLOWN CLOUDS*
(Escape Media Publishers 2003, Pilgrims Publishers 2013
City Lion Press 2019)

THE MASTER DIRECTOR:
A JOURNEY THROUGH POLITICS, DOUBT AND DEVOTION
WITH A HIMALAYAN MASTER
(HarperCollins 2014)

LEOPARD IN THE CITY
AN URBAN FABLE
(City Lion Press 2018)

Photography Books:

SCULPTURE GARDEN OF THE GODS
ANIMATED LANDSCAPE PHOTOGRAPHY FROM
THE GREEK ISLAND OF IKARIA
(City Lion Press 2018)

GANGES LAMENT
BLACK AND WHITE PHOTOGRAPHIC PORTRAITS FROM THE
SACRED INDIAN CITY OF VARANASI
(City Lion Press 2018)

Table of Contents

Photographs appear on the
Frontpiece and Page 112

Preface

This book tells the story of a journey I took in 1981, in my early twenties, to the Greek island of Corfu and to the stone monastery atop the island's highest mountain, a weather-beaten bare stone peak jutting out of the sea. I stayed there for a time with the old monk who had lived alone there for forty years.

As with all good things in life, journeys tend to be round, they circle round to their beginnings. This journey was no exception. One goes off, one comes home again, and then one reflects. This journey began and ended in Vermont. During the two years following my return, I spent most of my time writing about my experiences. I wrote the story through from the beginning to the end without stopping to revise or correct what I had written. The resulting manuscript of over six hundred typed and hand-written pages was the first draft of the pages that follow.

Both traveling and writing are bugs for which I have never found a cure. Before I had time to edit the manuscript and shape it for others to read, I was stricken again with the travel bug and set off on other travels. I left the manuscript with my sister, who lives in Washington DC, for safekeeping. When I returned from that journey, I wrote of other things, and quite got on with my life.

It was some years later that I started thinking about that old manuscript. I didn't necessarily want to work on it; I was merely curious. I only wanted to take a look. Like the Indian shopkeeper garnering customers off the street with the call, "Looking only, no buying," I thought I could simply take a peek. So I called my sister and asked her to send it.

My sister had been carefully guarding the manuscript all those years, and she was not keen to give it up to the US Postal Service. She reminded me that it was the only copy in existence and insisted on sending it by overnight express delivery.

I lived at the time at the end of a very long driveway off a dirt road that couriers often have difficulty finding. So, just to be safe, I had my sister send the manuscript in care of a friend, Kate Jones.

When I gave my sister the address, she said, "Kate Jones, what an unfortunate name."

I asked her what she meant.

"It's like Jane Doe," she said.

I assured her that Kate received overnight mail regularly and told her not to worry.

A week later Kate had received no package for me, so I called my sister again.

My sister lives a busy life. She apologized for forgetting to send the manuscript and promised again to send it right away. I must have only half believed her, for a good month went by and I hardly gave the manuscript a thought. Then it was her birthday and we were talking on the phone. I reminded her again, and this time she swore she would find the manuscript the moment she got off the phone and would send it the very next day.

It must have been nearly a week later that I called her again. I was beginning to grow tired of her promises and told her so. But she stopped me. She *had* sent it. It should have arrived four days earlier. She commented again on my friend's unfortunate name.

I called FedEx, and they tracked the package. The driver claimed he'd been unable to locate Kate's residence, so he'd done what he always did when he had difficulty locating someone in our area: he went to Sam's Septic Service. Since Sam emptied every septic tank in town, he knew precisely where everyone lived.

Sam told the driver that there was a K. Jones living just around the corner. He pointed out the apartment building.

The Kate Jones I know is my neighbor; she lives on a farm, miles away from the village.

But I knew the building Sam had referred to. It had long ago been nicknamed—by its residents, no less—the 'Brown Slum.' It is known for its transient and more down-and-out residents.

So the news couldn't have been worse. And as if that wasn't enough, he'd delivered it not to the K. Jones who lived there, but to a man loitering in front of the building that claimed to know her. He'd signed his name 'J. Miller.'

I was horrified.

I rushed down to the Brown Slum and started knocking on doors. The first door on which I knocked was opened by a man who worked the graveyard shift, and he was decidedly *not* happy to be awakened at nine-thirty in the morning. He said he had neither seen the package, nor had he heard of the man who'd signed for it, but he told me that indeed a woman named Jones did live in the building, though her name was not Kate, it was Kay. He pointed to the door across the hall. "She lives there," he said.

Kay Jones herself answered my knock. She had the pallid look of someone who hadn't seen the sun in years. The homemade tattoos that ran up and down her arms had a decidedly jailhouse look. She was haggard and tired, a woman worn to the bone by life's vicissitudes.

I pictured this woman opening my package on the off chance that it contained something of value, discovering only pages and pages of my barely legible scribbling, certainly worthless to her, and hiding it under a bed, or throwing it out so as not to be caught having opened someone else's mail.

She stood with the door half open, her hand clutching the doorknob, blocking entrance to her apartment. I explained why I was there.

"I never seen a package," she said, eyeing me closely.

I told her about J. Miller, who had signed for it.

"I never heard of no J. Miller," she said.

I had to think fast. If I assumed that she was lying, then my best chance was to make her sympathetic to my cause. So I launched into a long plea, explaining how the missing package contained the only copy of a manuscript I had spent years writing, and how it had no worth to anyone but me. She relaxed a bit and stepped back from the door, allowing me to enter her apartment.

Taking her into my confidence, I told her how I would understand if one of her *neighbors* had taken the package—just to see what was in it. I even said I might have done the same myself. I stressed that no questions would be asked. I even suggested that an anonymous phone call telling me the manuscript was sitting in a hall would suit me fine.

All I wanted was to have the manuscript back.

The entire time I was making my plea for help, I was moving around the room, trying to pick up some clue amidst piles of dirty clothes and overflowing bags of garbage. I was looking for the corner of a FedEx envelope, or a box of the right dimensions.

At first she was rather cold. I was, after all, barging into her apartment and basically accusing her of stealing my mail.

But how could anyone feel bad toward someone in my predicament?

Soon she was looking worried for me, especially when I told her that if it was truly gone I'd probably go mad and start banging my head against the closest wall.

What else could I say?

It was the truth.

Before the manuscript had been lost I was merely curious to see it. I had pictured myself flipping through the pages, cringing the whole while at my abuse of the English language, and perhaps recalling a few details of a journey that the years had swept from my mind.

But when I first heard the manuscript had not been delivered, its stock had risen a notch. And as the situation became more hopeless, I had even begun to see myself working on it again. Now that it was probably gone forever, I felt the full tragedy of its loss.

So I made a promise, a solemn vow. I vowed that if I could find the manuscript, I would complete it. I even believed the manuscript had become lost only to extract such a promise from me. I felt destiny at work.

I left my name and phone number with Kay Jones. That was all I could do. She promised to call if she heard anything.

Then I proceeded to knock on doors up and down the halls of the Brown Slum. At every door I repeated the entire story, left my phone number if they'd let me, and grew more desperate as the word *gone* rose like a lump in my throat.

By the time I reached the last door, and delivered my story for the umpteenth time, this time to a middle-aged woman dressed in an old coffee-stained bathrobe, I was entirely discouraged and thoroughly depressed. Still I tried to remain upbeat.

But it was no use. Halfway through my impassioned plea the phone rang. The woman answered it and started arguing with a man from a collection agency. He was threatening her with court and jail and worse if she didn't come up with a certain sum in short order. "I have no money," she said, "especially none to give you!" She argued desperately for a good ten minutes while I stood in the doorway. Finally I gave up.

I went back outside and started walking away. None of the people to whom I'd made my plea seemed likely to go out of their way to help.

I went over again what must have happened. Someone must have gotten their hands on the package, (most likely Kay Jones but there was no telling), and thrown it away.

Then it hit me: if so, it would probably have ended up in the tenement's dumpster.

I went to the parking lot, lifted the dumpster's lid, and was almost blown off my feet by the stench of death. Holding my nose, afraid of what I might find, I looked inside.

There on top of dozens of plastic bags of trash were the remains of a slaughtered pig. Huge ball joints—the cartilage still white and glistening—leg bones, and whole sides of fat—from which, under happier circumstances, bacon would be cut—were all draped over the shiny black bags, slowly decaying beneath a thick cloud of flies that rose when I opened the lid, then settled again on their quarry.

Holding both my breath and my nose, I looked beneath the carnage for something resembling a box of paper. But I saw no such box. I thought of ripping the bags open, but the festering pig flesh and the flies turned my stomach.

I could not endure it.

So I closed the dumpster and walked away, riling against the fate of having lost the manuscript at precisely the moment I realized its importance. I tried to get used to the fact that I would never see the manuscript again.

I couldn't.

That dumpster was my only chance.

I found a broken broom handle lying underneath a bush and returned to the scene of the carnage. I opened the dumpster again, held my breath, and started poking the bags of trash, ripping them open, and trying to see what lay beneath.

I worked my way systematically through the dumpster, from one side to the other. When I reached the farthest corner and moved the very last bag of garbage I spied a plastic grocery bag tied shut around something the size of a ream of paper. Catching the handle with the stick, I moved the bag to the side. Then I held my breath, leaned deep into the dumpster, and snatched it out.

I opened the bag and there it was, hundreds of typed and handwritten pages that I hadn't seen in a decade. Someone had ripped open the box, taken the pages out, shuffled through them, and then stuffed the whole mess into the bag. Every single page was there.

Having literally saved the manuscript from the jaws of death, I walked away from that dumpster clutching the plastic bag to my breast.

And so it was I had no choice but to finish the project I had begun so long ago.

Chapter 1

I was on a ferryboat making a night crossing of the Adriatic Sea, from the southern Italian port of Brindisi to the Greek island of Corfu, where I had lived before. The sun was about to rise and I was leaning against the rail, straining for sight of land, confounding clouds on the horizon for mountains. The bow sliced through the calm, dark sea, peeling back wave after wave, each tinged with the glow of the eastern sky.

The mountains only appeared when they were quite close, their peaks having been hidden in the clouds, both cloud and rock having been washed pink by the early dawn light. The rising sun dispersed the clouds, leaving the rock gray against a blue sky.

The sun had risen fully by the time we drew close to land. The mountains were too high and wild to be Corfu's. We were off the coast of Albania. Nowhere had I seen mountains as rugged as these. We steamed south and entered a strait between an island and the mainland. As we rounded the island's northern shore I searched for some sign by which I could know the island was Corfu and not some other. For so long I had been traveling through unknown lands, never seeing a familiar sight, never pausing long enough to grow accustomed to a single face, forever the stranger passing through.

Villages of whitewashed houses lay nestled along the green strip of shore. Behind the villages the land rose to steep mountains. Following the stony slopes up from the coast, a spark of recognition shot through me as I saw one final towering peak, a stony cone I would have recognized anywhere as belonging to Corfu's northern mountains. Seeing that mountain was like seeing an old friend.

ə   ə

When the boat docked I was the first one off, leading two dozen other disembarking passengers down the pier and toward the customs building. Opening the door to a long, wide corridor of low customs inspection tables, I realized there wasn't an inspector in sight. The boat had docked a few minutes early, probably catching them on their morning coffee break. Knowing they were supposed to be picking out the more suspicious of us for inspection, I wondered whether it was all right to pass through so blithely. But I was excited to be back on Corfu. I strode on as determinedly as a tour-guide leading his innocent charges.

I swung open the door to the noisy waiting room, but before I could take another step, a large and imposing customs man, standing two inches in front of my face, blocked my advance. I stopped, shocked by his sudden appearance. The suitcase belonging to the lady behind me jabbed into my ribs.

The customs official had a big black mustache, a chest full of medals, and stripes on his shoulders to prove his authority. He spoke English with a thick Greek accent. "Where you come from?" he demanded.

"Italy," I replied.

"How you get here?"

"On that boat," and I pointed to it.

"Oh!" he said, and his face lit up. He tipped his hat. "Welcome to Corfu!"

I returned his beaming smile and bounded through the waiting room, leaving the others far behind. Corfu hadn't changed. I was ready to let its magic once again wash over me.

Making my way through the clamor, I cut inland onto the narrow, winding streets and alleys. An old woman riding sidesaddle on a donkey came toward me. She smiled and said, "*Kali mera,*" good morning, as we passed. Young children in blue uniforms, eyes big as almonds, went by like schools of tiny fish. An old man sat on a chair by his door with a coat thrown over his shoulders, a cup of Greek coffee balanced on his knee, and a cigarette in his hand. He smiled as I passed. His smile wasn't

forced, it wasn't put on, it wasn't even polite: it was the smile of someone alive to the morning, greeting the sun and the new day—as well as
passers-by.

Every sight, smell, and sound brought back memories; past experiences flashed through my mind like crystals forming around a nucleus. I
recalled the first time I'd arrived on Corfu six years earlier. I was making
the same passage from Italy to Greece, only that time I was headed to
the boat's final destination, the city of Patras on the Greek mainland,
from where I would go by bus to Athens. I had met some other travelers
on the boat and we had talked late into the night. Long after the moon
had sunk below the horizon, I had fallen asleep on a bench on deck. The
boat wasn't due to dock at Patras till afternoon.

The next thing I knew the sun was beating on my closed eyelids. I
heard the tooting of a car horn. I heard the braying of a donkey. In the
distance voices were raised in song. I opened my eyes to see hillsides
covered by whitewashed buildings shining brilliantly in the sun. Passengers stood around me, looking at the town and waving good-bye to
people on shore. Sailors were loosening the ropes, and I realized I had
but seconds to get off the boat. Running down the gangplank, I jumped
to shore just as the gangplank was raised.

Clearing customs, and still half-asleep, I stumbled onto the street
and stepped unwittingly into a parade. I had arrived on the morning of
Greece's highest holiday, the Orthodox Easter.

The parade was a magnificent affair, with priests in their finest black
robes followed by musicians and singers. Then came dancers dressed in
traditional costumes. Children shook loose from their parents and joined
the growing procession, many leading goats and sheep. Everyone was
being swept into the parade, and I couldn't help being swept up as well.

Noticing that some of my companions from the boat had also joined
the parade, I asked if any of them knew where to get the bus for Athens.
They laughed at me when they realized I wasn't kidding. To my dumb
stare they explained that we were on an island and that the island's name
was Corfu. The boat's *next* stop was the mainland. I had never heard of

Corfu before, but what I had seen of it so far, I liked.

Peter, a wiry Englishman, had been to Corfu before. He suggested we all go to Kontókali, a village up the coast some five miles away, where he knew of a taverna with rooms to rent. So we went, four or five of us, to Kontókali.

After settling in, we borrowed bicycles and took a ride down a dirt road through a grove of olive trees. We came upon an old van parked off the side of the road in the shade of a huge olive tree. Bouzouki music blared from the radio, and an old man with a glass in one hand and a cane in the other signaled us over by waving his cane above his head.

A party consisting of a huge family, ranging from an old woman wearing a weathered peasant dress to her great-grandchildren who were barely old enough to walk, were having their Easter dinner. They invited us to join them. We hadn't a language in common but that mattered little: this was a day of festivity, celebrating the risen Christ.

The old man handed each of us a small glass filled to the brim with ouzo, Greece's clear, anise-flavored liquor. He motioned us to empty our glasses in a single gulp, which we each did in turn while the others cheered and laughed. We repeated this ritual three or four times until the old woman snatched the bottle from his hand. She was afraid we'd be unable to ride our bicycles home. After breaking bread with them and having a meal of spit-roasted lamb, rice, bread, feta, and olives, someone turned up the music, and we attempted to learn Greek dances under the twisted boughs of the olive trees. We were not very good pupils: the ouzo was still coursing through our veins. We staggered more than danced. With hugs and laughter, we mounted our bicycles and rode back to Kontókali.

Corfu is a world set apart. Time moves with a lazy fluidity, and magic sweeps through the air. It is a land where anything can and constantly does happen. My first visit there stretched into a two-month-long stay. I rented a house in the hills outside Kontókali with one of the people from the boat. We rarely planned what we would do from one day to the next; it was enough to allow the events of the day to come to us. It was to the same house that I was now headed. Now, my brother Andy and his wife Ann lived there.

☙   ❧

The course I took through the streets of Corfu Town was determined by no particular rationale; recollection and intuition were my sole guides. I had never completely mastered navigation in Corfu Town; I knew portions of the town as the New Port, the Old Port, the market street near the Church of Saint Spyrodon, and the bus square. Winding, narrow streets connected these places. When to go right and when to go left were decisions made spontaneously. Often it was a slight detail that triggered recognition, a place where the road turned to cobbles or where an old woman fed stray cats. I knew the town not entirely, but intimately.

Near the bus stop in Corfu Town was a small dairy and bakeshop, a place I had thought of often since I'd last left Corfu. I had often sat at a corner table for an hour or more eating a raisin bun and a bowl of *crema,* a goat milk pudding, watching old Greek men talking and smoking and telling jokes. The place had an atmosphere akin to a family hearth. Walking through the narrow streets, I remembered Spiros, the elderly proprietor who presided over the scene with the kindness and concern of a shepherd. He was a large man with protruding eyes. Stretched taut over his ample frame, his skin was as pale as the milk he sold.

Inside the bakeshop, above the money box, behind the high glass counter of milk and cheeses in the back, was a small alcove shrine. It was a dark corner, seemingly arising out of mystery itself. In this shrine the olive oil lamps were always sputtering and illuminating the icons of Christ the Shepherd and the Virgin holding the babe in her arms. The lamps also illuminated pictures of Spiros' parents, wife, and children. As I sped through the streets, I wondered whether the shop and the shrine were still there after all these years.

To my delight, the bakeshop was right where it was supposed to be. I ducked inside. The corner table—*my* table—was free. I sat. Nothing had changed. There was Spiros sitting on his stool behind the glass case.

Above his head was the shrine, glowing warmly. It was as if the scene had been frozen in time. I ordered a raisin bun and *crema*.

After breakfast, I rounded the corner to the bus square and took the bus to Kontókali to see my brother and sister-in-law. Arriving in the village, I found the well-trodden path that led through olive groves and bamboo enclosures for sheep. It passed through the little farm where pigs, chickens, and turkeys all roamed free. Then it entered another grove of olive trees, their trunks all twisted and gnarled with age. At the far end of this grove stood the house, suffused with an atmosphere of inviting dereliction. Ancient trees overhung its clay-tiled roof; whitewash peeled from its walls; plaster crumbled to reveal the stone beneath; the shutters were broken. The house looked the same as it had when I'd first set eyes on it years before. Living in this house was like living in a ruin; one constantly uncovered relics from the past.

Since Andy and Ann had no idea I was coming, I approached the house stealthily to surprise them. The front door was locked. So was the back. I tried all the windows, but the house was locked up tight. I sat down in the grass under the tumbling grape arbor by the front door. Then I lay down. I was tired. I kept wondering whether they could have left the island. Perhaps they had gone away for a few days. These were my last thoughts as my eyelids grew heavy and I fell into a deep sleep.

I awoke with a start to find a donkey peering down at me and sniffing my face. An old woman held its leather lead, and I recognized her as the woman who lived in the house farther up the path. Somehow, her name flashed in my mind.

"Lefteria!" I called out as I jumped to my feet, startling the donkey. "Lefteria!" I called again. Lefteria was visibly shocked that I knew her name.

"Andy? Ann?" I said and pointed at the house.

A puzzled look crossed her face. Then she brightened and said, "Ah, Andreas, Anna," and she launched into a rapid and fiery monologue, gesticulating so emphatically that she upset the donkey, who started braying plaintively.

When she finished I rejoined with an equally long and rambling story of how I had come to the house only to find no one home and had been worried that they had gone or were called away because of emergency, but felt better now that she had known their names and didn't seem to be implying that they were gone. I used especially obscure words and complicated ways of saying things to heighten the sense of the absurd I felt at having such an earnest discussion with this woman, whose vocabulary and my own coincided only on the words *Andreas* and *Anna*.

When I finished my side of the story she shrugged her shoulders. A smile crossed her lips. Then we both burst out laughing. She dug deep into her pocket and took out a handful of ripe figs. She gave me half, called to her donkey, and they continued up the path toward her house.

I fell back asleep and awoke when the sun was much higher in the sky. This time I awoke from familiar voices calling out my name. I jumped to my feet, Andy and Ann dropped their groceries, and we hugged one another. "How long have you been here?" they asked. "Where were you? I thought you had left," I said, and we all bubbled over with questions and answers. It had been a long time since we had seen one another and there was much catching up to do.

Chapter 2

Within a few days we fell into a routine akin to the languid ways of Corfu itself. The house was surrounded with fruit trees over-laden with ripe fruit—figs and apples, oranges and lemons, pears, cactus fruit, and berries—and no matter how much we ate, even more fell to the ground to rot.

The first one up in the morning would find the tree that had the largest and most ripe figs and pick a small basketful to spread on the breakfast toast, which we made by holding bread with a fork over a gas burner.

On Mondays, Wednesdays, and Fridays we took the bus to Corfu Town. On these days Ann, the only one of us who spoke Greek, gave an English lesson to the daughter of the people who owned a small vegetable shop where we shopped. While Ann gave her lesson, Andy and I went shopping.

It was often humorous, Andy and I pushing our way through the crowd of Greek mamas at the bake shop, trying to get the attention of the man behind the counter, handicapped by language, knowing only a set formula of three words to yell out to get the loaf we wanted. "*Ena mavro psomi.*" Those were the magic words, "One dark bread," and the man would weigh and wrap our whole wheat bread, then write a number on a scrap of paper to tell us the price. That was usually our first stop, after which we'd go to the vegetable shop where the couple whose daughter Ann was then teaching would greet us at the door to help us pick out our vegetables. Then we were off to the fish street, a narrow cobbled alleyway where fishmongers in tiny stalls sold yesterday's catch from wooden bins. We were usually after the small, minnow-like fish that the fishermen attract to their boats at night with gas lanterns hung off the boats' sterns. One could see the boats at night on the mirror-calm water of the harbor, points of bright light in a sea of darkness. We'd point to these fish and say, "Ten grams" (which is very little), and they in turn would laugh at us until we explained, "*Gato,*" for the cat. Sometimes they gave us the fish for free. Then we'd go to the dry-goods store for rice, noodles, soap, and toilet paper.

We usually rushed through our shopping so we'd be free to go to the *kafeneon*—or coffee house—that we dubbed the Chess Café, where we'd play chess and drink coffee until Ann was through giving the lesson.

The Chess Café, much like the bake and dairy shop I had rushed to on my first day back on Corfu, was a place in which old Greek men spent most of their waking hours drinking coffee, beer, or brandy, smoking cigarettes, and playing cards. Two or three heated games were always under way.

Greeks play cards like no other people I've seen. When it is his turn to put a card down, the Greek doesn't merely pick a card from his hand and put it on the table. He lets a good chunk of time lapse first. He deliberates so long and hard that all eyes are trained on him. Then he chooses a card from his hand with a look on his face that says he'll win the game in a single blow. He holds the card high over the middle of the table and lets his hand quiver before he slaps it onto the table with a loud snap and grunts as if to say, 'So there!' Then he quickly looks around the table to judge reaction, which invariably is loud and raucous. Never sure whether the reactions were due to the particular card slapped down or to the quality of the delivery, the game they played always eluded me. As far as I could judge, the rules were constantly changing, and cheating was an integral part of winning.

One day, Andy and I were playing chess, and Andy was taking a long time to move—I had just threatened his queen and he was looking for a way out without loosing his knight. I happened to be watching the card game at the center table, which had become quite rowdy, when one of the players stood up to go to the toilet. The moment the man closed the toilet door the others grew mischievous. Looking like a gang of eight-year-olds, they picked up the stack of cards before the empty seat and quickly rearranged them, placing them back on the table just as the door opened and their friend walked over, adjusting his fly. The looks that flashed around the table were priceless as the poor man lost hand after hand, and finally lost the game in disgust. Then they dealt another hand, and they slapped cards down on the table a few more rounds until another of the players went to the toilet. Once again, the moment he shut the door behind himself the others rearranged his cards and returned them just in time. The game resumed and the next victim of the rouse lost miserably, completely unsuspecting of the antics he had participated in only moments before.

The Chess Café was the perfect place for a game of chess. One moment Andy and I would be engrossed in the world of bishops, queens, and pawns, and the next we would be watching the card player's antics, or the son of the café's owner taking a metal tray of Greek coffee, tea, and ouzo to a shop owner down the street.

Our game was usually in its final stages when Ann arrived from her lesson. We'd have another coffee with her before leaving, and then make a few more stops to purchase items that Andy and I had been unable to buy without her linguistic assistance. After shopping, we would take the bus back to Kontókali, and by the time we were walking up the path into the hills, the sun would be so intense that we'd feel ready to die from the heat. But we would counter the heat by going to the well to pour buckets of cool water over our heads. After a lunch of bread, feta, tomatoes, onions, and olives would come a nap, necessary in such a hot climate.

Our days were, to put it plainly, lazy and idyllic. We were living in a paradise where our needs were both few, and easily met. Things were so perfect that they couldn't possibly last that way, though at the time we were naïve enough to think they could.

❧   ❧

Andy and Ann first met on Corfu many years earlier and had now lived there together for over a year. After a few years back in the States they had returned to Corfu, hoping to live on the island permanently. The only way they could stay on the island was to acquire residence permits, and the only way to do that was to start a small business. Since Ann knew how to weave they decided to start a small weaving business, consisting of a loom and Ann sitting at it, making rugs and wall hangings to be sold at tourist shops in Corfu Town. It wasn't exactly a front—they *did* hope to gain a little income from the business—but what they really wanted was their residence permits.

When I arrived, they were ready to start. The only thing holding them back was the rain that fell with too much regularity in Ioánnina, a town across the strait in the mountains of the mainland known for its wool. They had bought wool in Ioánnina and arranged for someone to dye it. But the dyer could only dye the wool during a long stretch of dry weather; for after dunking the wool into the dye, he'd have to hang it outside, and if it didn't dry quickly the dye wouldn't set.

We always thought it odd that Ioánnina should be receiving so much rain while Corfu was in the middle of its dry season; but Ioánnina was, after all, in the mountains. And in Greece such details as these, or delays of a few weeks, don't mean what they do elsewhere. If you hold someone to a deadline in Greece he often becomes indignant, as if you are breaking a code of Greek ethics. Just to spite you he'll slow down even more to prove the point. It is a matter of survival to accede and say, "If it's not done today, maybe next week it'll be done, or the week after that." In the meantime you continue picking your morning figs and taking afternoon walks through the olive groves.

In order to receive their permits to start a business, Andy and Ann had made a deep incursion into the labyrinthine world of Greek bureaucracy. Every weekday morning for the past three months they had presented themselves before a man in uniform they called—in mock affection—the 'Main Man.' Pinned to his chest was a badge surrounded by medals, and perched on his head was a crisp military cap. The Main Man worked out of police headquarters in Corfu Town.

A police headquarters in Greece is usually the last place you want end up. It wasn't that long before that the country was run by the colonels, during whose regime the police were the long arm of the colonels' dictatorial rule and were notorious for their nefarious ways. In those days, the police struck terror in the hearts of villagers and city-dwellers alike, enforcing the will of the colonels with gleeful and vicious abandon. And when they weren't busy fulfilling the colonels' will, they were busy imposing their own on whomever they saw fit. Local police chiefs held the same arbitrary terror over their villages as the colonels held over the country.

Now the colonels were gone, replaced by an elected government. But through this change of government many of the police had kept their posts. The same hated men to whom the colonels had given free rein were now supposedly reined in by Parliament. But they still had tricks hidden up their sleeves, and evil schemes hatched in their brains. Their specialty was finding obscure laws to bring down their enemies.

One such law stated that every restaurant had to have a bathroom and that every bathroom had to have toilet paper. The penalty for running out of toilet paper was swift and severe: the police would instantly impound the restaurant and throw the owner in jail. This law struck terror in the heart of every restaurateur, for with this law the police could close down whomever they didn't like. The police were not above removing toilet paper from a bathroom and then conducting a raid. So restaurant owners who had spoken out against the colonels when they had killed the students at the university in Athens, or who didn't like giving free food to the police, or whose family had a land dispute dating back five generations with a policeman's family—all these restaurateurs had to protect themselves against toilet paper raids, which they did by filling their tiny bathrooms with cases of toilet paper. You could tell a restaurant owner's standing with the police by the amount of toilet paper in his bathroom. Sometimes you could hardly open the door, much less fit yourself inside and close the door behind you. Needless to say, one approached the police with caution.

Every day at nine o'clock sharp, Andy and Ann presented themselves at police headquarters well scrubbed and in clean clothes. The Main Man, despite his military demeanor and questionable background, was not, in the end, all that bad. From him they received their instructions. He would tell them which government office to go to for a particular form. Invariably, they'd have to take that form to another bureaucratic office for the signature of some functionary. The signed form would then have to go to a third office to be stamped. Every stage of their journey would entail a fee, some of which were legitimate, others not, though of course one never asked and therefore never knew. They learned early on to follow the Main Man's instructions to the letter and to complete all the steps he laid out in the morning before the fall of night. They learned this one day when they became tired of government offices and decided to go back to Kontókali before getting the final stamp on the day's form. They figured they could do it the next day. But the next day they discovered the form had to be signed and stamped the same day it was issued. They had to start all over, wasting a day and paying all the fees twice. So they followed the Main Man's directions carefully, and in the end he was really quite helpful. He even pointed them in the direction of a good lawyer who pled their case for a business license before the district court.

It all went off without a hitch. All their forms were signed, stamped, duplicated, notarized, and blessed—all, that is, except one, the one that had to go to Athens for approval. That form was their residence permit. Since their business permit was approved and in hand, and since the Main Man considered the residence permits a mere formality, he said that as far as he was concerned they could start working. That was when they started designing and building their loom and traveling to Ioánnina to order wool, the wool they were waiting for when I arrived.

So the days wore on. Andy and Ann waited for their wool, as I awaited the next step on my journey. Limbo is fine as long as there is something at the other end to pull you out; I was continually trying to figure out just what that something might be. I was considering where to spend the winter, and thought of possibly going to Crete or Turkey or North Africa. But as I considered each of these places I found myself gazing at Corfu's northern mountains, the same mountains that I had seen as the ferryboat rounded Corfu's northern shore. My thoughts of far away lands were continually preempted by speculations about these mountains.

Corfu is roughly hourglass-shaped, a narrow isthmus in the middle, widening both north and south. In the north are the island's only mountains. And these mountains rise toward a single stony peak, the highest point on the island, the mountain Pantokrator.

Corfu is one of Greece's most lush islands. But Corfu's mountains rise to an altitude that can support only bare and naked rock. The mountains stand solidly contrasted against both the deep blue sky and the verdant lowlands. The mountains are so massive that no matter where you are on the island, if you look up, there they are.

This omnipresence might not have struck everyone, but I was fairly hounded by it. I would catch myself staring up at the naked face of Pantokrator, daydreaming, imagining life amid so much stone. But the strangest thing was what I was thinking of when I caught my gaze directed upon those rocky peaks. Invariably I would be considering my further travels. I would be in the bus, for instance, coming back from Corfu Town with bags of vegetables on my lap thinking about going to North Africa, considering the relative cost of flying to taking a boat. Then I'd realize I was staring across the bay at the mountains, distracted from thoughts of North Africa, wondering instead what it was like in those mountains. Or in the olive grove above the house where I would sometimes take solitary walks, and where inevitably my thoughts would turn to where I would go next, I often stopped in a little meadow. A huge rock stood in the meadow that I liked to sit on. I would look down the hill toward the coast and dream of distant lands. And, in fact, I'd been going up there a long time before I realized that from that rock an opening in the trees offered an unobstructed view of the mountain Pantokrator. And I even discovered that the very tip of the mountain was visible just above a rooftop when one looked out the window of the Chess Café.

The very ease of life in Kontókali, though seductive, couldn't hold me; in fact it compelled me to consider moving on. Had I stayed there, I'm afraid I would have grown stagnant. I knew it was merely a point of rest from which I would launch my next move. Yet, no matter how much I thought of traveling to some distant shore, Corfu's northern mountains were calling. It was an uncanny feeling, one probably best described as intuition. It was a call I did my best to resist. I fully intended to leave the island. I was pricing tickets to Africa. I was trying to imagine myself in Istanbul. But as if some unseen hand were turning my head and pointing, or as if the mountain hid in its bulk a lodestone to which I alone responded, it became increasingly difficult for me to deny the call.

Chapter 3

It actually took some time for me to heed the mountain's call; in the mean time I was content to live in Kontókali in what was almost a state of suspended animation, watching the hot, dry days of summer turn into the cooler, wet days of fall.

The sky had been cloudless for so many months that when the clouds came, they built over the course of a week, slowly blotting out the deep blue sky by day, and by night obliterating the stars one by one. Each day threatened rain more than the last until the clouds became so heavy with dark, threatening moisture that they could hold it no longer. The sky cracked open and released a deluge on Corfu.

The threat of rain had hung over us so long that when it finally came it was a relief. But for us that relief was short lived, for when the rain fell we discovered our roof leaked. The worst leaks were right over Andy and Ann's bed. We had to move their bed and place buckets under the drips. The roof leaked elsewhere as well. We employed every bucket and pan in our possession.

On our way to town the next day we stopped in the village to see our landlord Giorgos. The house had been in his family for generations. Giorgos, his father, and grandfather had all been born there, and they had all lived there until Giorgos had bought a house in the village some ten years earlier and moved the family from the hill. When we told Giorgos about the roof he was apologetic. His wife Maria was concerned we'd all catch cold. Giorgos promised to find a roofer and get right to it.

A week later, after a few more rainfalls, we went to see Giorgos again. He was now a little less eager. He told us he was having trouble finding a roofer. Because the house was so old, he explained, and since tiles were missing, the beams under the tiles were sure to be rotten. He needed to find not only a roofer—there were plenty of roofers—but a small roofer, one whose weight wouldn't crush the beams as he crawled across them. "I must find a jockey-sized roofer," he said.

A few days later we were lounging under the grape arbor in front of the house, sipping coffee after awakening from a nap, when we saw Giorgos coming up the path through the olive grove accompanied by a man no more than four-and-a-half feet tall. They each held an end of a long wooden ladder.

Overjoyed at their arrival, we offered them coffee and ouzo; but Giorgos was all business. He must have been paying the roofer by the hour. We showed them where the roof was at its worst, over Andy and Ann's bedroom. They leaned the ladder against the building and Andy held the bottom of the ladder steady. The roofer climbed the ladder, Ann pointed out to Giorgos where the leaks were, and Giorgos shouted instructions to the roofer. The roofer took off a few tiles and stuck his head in through the hole.

What would have happened had Andy not been holding the ladder, I don't know. It probably would have been the end of the jockey-sized roofer. For whatever lay in that hole caused him to recoil so violently that he surely would have tipped the ladder back. He let out a string of curses. Immediately, I thought of hornets. But as he didn't flee down the ladder it couldn't have been that kind of danger. The condition of the roof must have horrified him. Or maybe something had died in there. Carefully, he put his head back through the hole, and there he stood for the longest time, his head under the tiles, transfixed by what he saw. When he came back down he was ashen and shaking like a leaf. He pulled Giorgos to one side and whispered something in his ear. Giorgos knitted his bushy brows.

"No!" Giorgos said in disbelief.

"Yes!" the roofer insisted. "See for yourself."

Giorgos climbed the ladder and repeated the roofer's long, steady stare. When he came down, he too looked shaken, and quickly took the ladder away from the house.

Giorgos told us the roof was extremely dangerous. He said it could fall at any moment. He kept repeating the word *epikinthunos,* dangerous. The roofer agreed so strenuously that I thought his head might fall off his neck from nodding so forcefully. They said that Andy and Ann should take all their possessions out of the room and close the door behind them.

"Do not return to that room," Giorgos said, his voice quivering with emotion. And with that Giorgos and the roofer hoisted the ladder over their shoulders and set off down the path toward the village.

We thought it odd that the roof, after so many years of slow deterioration, should suddenly be in such danger of collapse—in fact, Giorgos and the roofer's reaction seemed more than just odd: it was really bizarre. We decided the repair job must have been beyond both their expectations and their abilities. This bothered us because instead of fixing the roof, Giorgos would be all the more likely to evoke that Greek turn of mind that says, *If it isn't done today, maybe next week*, and we'd be left emptying buckets and mopping the floor.

Meanwhile, Andy and Ann were becoming tired of waiting for the wool. Ann had some rather nasty exchanges with the wool dyer in Ioánnina. It became a new part of our routine: after shopping and chess and coffee, we'd stop off at the long-distance telephone exchange and Ann would call the wool dyer, a conversation that invariably ended in shouting—and no wool.

And I? I was busy studying maps of the northern mountains. At the base of the highest mountain, Pantokrator, which appeared uninhabited, was the village of Strinilas, the highest village on the island. I thought a mountain village would be a good place to live quietly and do some writing. So I decided to find a small house to rent in Strinilas for the winter.

One day in town, after shopping and before going to the Chess Café, I went to inquire about buses to Strinilas. I had bought a small book entitled *Beginning Greek,* which I had been going over with Ann. I was always looking for opportunities to practice my Greek, and I thought a trip to the inquiries office would offer a great opportunity. I worked out exactly what to say, rehearsed it in my mind repeatedly, and walked up to the window. I gave my spiel, which in translation went simply, "When bus Strinilas?" (I've never been good at foreign languages). The clerk—he was actually a boy, no more than seventeen—answered in perfect English. "There are buses on Tuesdays, Thursdays, and Saturdays leaving Corfu at five forty-five in the morning and returning from Strinilas at nine-fifteen. Another bus leaves Corfu at one-thirty on those days and returns at four-thirty."

Although crestfallen at a lost opportunity to practice my fledgling Greek, I was glad for the information. I walked to the Chess Café where Andy was waiting for me. I told him I was going to Strinilas the next day on the morning bus, and would return in the afternoon.

That afternoon, after eating lunch, we sat on the front step of our little house sipping coffee. Andy and Ann were discussing whether or not to go to Ioánnina to see if it really rained there. Half listening to their conversation, I gazed through the trees at the mountain Pantokrator. Suddenly they stopped talking, and I saw that they were both staring down the path. It was Giorgos. But this time he came not with the jockey-sized roofer. This time, two uniformed policemen accompanied him. Panic flashed through each of us. What could they want? We were quickly working out alibis for crimes we had not committed in places we had never been when we noticed that the police were carrying over their shoulders the long wooden ladder.

Placing the ladder against the outside wall of the bedroom, Giorgos climbed slowly, as if he thought any quick movement might cause the roof to cave in. He peered inside, as he had the first time, then he came back down. Each of the policemen took his turn at what was beginning to look like a ritual: to climb the ladder carefully, peer inside through the hole in the tiles with the utmost concentration, and then climb slowly back down. Each took his turn; each went up twice. They refused to let any of us take a look. As they took the ladder away from the roof,

Giorgos reiterated that we were not even to go into the room. We were to remove all of our belongings and shut the door.

"Do not open the door again," he said gravely.

"Stay out of that room!" the policemen concurred.

Then they lifted the ladder onto their shoulders and walked through the olive grove toward the village. They left us more mystified than before, wondering whether the roof would be fixed before the end of the rainy season.

Chapter 4

Next morning I awoke well before sunrise and ate a substantial break-fast. Then I put together a lunch of bread, feta, tomatoes, and olives. The last sliver of a waning moon lit my way down the path to the village.

I hoped to flag down the bus to Strinilas when it came through Kontókali on its way north along the coast. This was not easy since at five forty-five in the morning a whole fleet of buses left Corfu for points north along the coast road. I had but a split second to discern the un-lit destination sign—written in Greek lettering—before the bus rushed past. After flagging down two wrong buses, the Strinilas bus finally came and stopped for me.

As I ran to the front door, a young man stuck his head out the win-dow reserved for the ticket collector. He yelled to me in English, "Hello, friend, do you remember me?" But it was too dark to see who he was. I jumped on the bus and it sped off. The ticket collector got up and insist-ed I sit in his seat so I could better see the countryside that we would be passing through. He sat on the vibrating motor cover between my seat and the driver's. "You don't remember me," he said. Although I knew we had met, I had to admit I didn't know where. "You came into the bus station yesterday," he said, "and tried to ask in Greek about the buses to Strinilas. You looked very upset when I answered in English." He told the story to the driver and they both had a good laugh.

We followed the coast road to the north of the island, and just as the sky was beginning to lighten in the east, and the mountains of Albania were becoming visible in the distance, we cut inland on a road that switched back and forth through groves of olive trees. We had entered the mountains.

Olive trees, with their slender silver-gray leaves, are particularly beautiful and mysterious during the early morning hours. The trunk of an olive tree resembles more a collection of thick vines interwoven and grown together than a solid and unified trunk. Even in the oldest trees there are passages to the center of the trunk, and sometimes you can see clear through to the other side. If ever there was a tree meant to be inhabited by tree spirits, it is the olive tree, with its ancient secret chambers.

Above the olive groves the terrain became steeper, and the road—obviously built long before the advent of buses—became narrow, the turns too tight for the bus to negotiate in a single attempt. At the first such turn, the driver spun the wheel and nosed the bus up to the rock face that the road cut into the mountain. Then the ticket collector ran to the back of the bus, looked out the back window, and yelled, "*Éla, éla, éla,*" come, come, come. He guided the bus back to the very edge of the road, which dropped off precipitously. Then he yelled, "*Endáxi,*" enough, just as we felt the rear wheels start to plunge. Then the driver rounded the corner and moved to the next turn.

We were traveling through an increasingly rugged and wild landscape devoid of settlements when a peasant woman, who was sitting upon bulging burlap sacks with a kerchief tied around her head, flagged down the bus. As the driver stopped for her, it was obvious that the sacks were too heavy for her to lift. The ticket collector and I helped her onto the bus, and then we hauled the bags on for her. She hadn't any shoes and her dress was dirty, as if she had been working in a nearby field all night. Sitting on the floor by the door and looking around the bus, she began to laugh for no apparent reason. Her eyes sparkled, perhaps betraying a slight madness. She took some nuts out of one pocket of her dress and a rock out of another. She used the rock to smash the nuts open on the floor of the bus.

Soon we came upon a few small farmhouses made of gray rock with red tiled roofs. Chickens, goats, turkeys, pigs, and donkeys all ran free on the road. Then we passed a small school. We were entering the village of Spartilas. We stopped in the village center, across from a *kafeneon*.

The ticket collector and I helped the old woman off the bus then leaned her sacks against a building. Plopping herself upon one of the sacks, she started laughing again at nothing in particular.

The driver, a burly man with a large and fleshy nose, invited the ticket collector and me to have a coffee. Inside the *kafeneon*, the driver bellowed to the man behind the counter, "Coffee for me and my friends." And when we were through with our coffee he bellowed again, "Ouzo. My friends want ouzo." When the man came with a bottle and three glasses, both the ticket collector and I declined. Greedily gulping down the ouzo, the driver smacked his lips and yelled out, "Ouzo. More ouzo!" The ticket collector was standing by now. He lifted the driver out of his seat and told the *kafeneon* owner, who was approaching with the bottle, to give him no more. To the obvious relief of the ticket collector, the driver didn't put up a struggle. As the driver took out a large note and paid the bill, the ticket collector told me that the driver had a problem with ouzo. "They like me to go with him on his route," he told me, "because he is my uncle, and though no one can make him stop drinking entirely, at least I can make him stop after one drink. Last month he crashed a bus."

When we stepped back onto the street, the whitewashed houses and shops of Spartilas, perched precariously on the side of the mountain, were bathed in the pink glow of the morning sun. Far below and in the distance, Corfu Town shone like a white, multi-faceted jewel. Near Kontókali, where my morning's journey had begun, I could see fishing boats setting out for the strait between the island and Albania. It was all so far away, yet I could see it all so clearly. A feeling of lucidity came over me. I knew this day would bare much fruit.

Above the village the landscape changed dramatically. It was here that the island's lush green growth gave way to the browns and grays of earth and bare stone. We passed a few farms, but they were no longer situated among flowers and fruit trees. These farms had an increasingly desolate look. The few trees that grew above Spartilas were stunted and gnarled. The livestock were lean. We passed a shepherd surrounded by his flock, the sheep grazing off the stunted brush growing out of crevices and fissures. The shepherd raised his staff in greeting as we passed.

A few miles above Spartilas, we turned right onto an even smaller road that ran along a shelf cut out of the side of the mountain. There were no houses or farms on this road; there were few signs of life at all, only a short black stubble where bushes had once grown but had been claimed by wildfires that frequented the mountains and terrorized the few mountain villages in the hot, dry summers. From the coast, one sees these fires as glowing red lines moving up the mountain slopes.

The village of Strinilas appeared, nestled in a fold of the mountain Pantokrator. As the bus passed the first few houses on the village's out-skirts it became clear that life in this village was not easy. The stone houses, thick walled and solid, stout and low to the ground, were built to withstand wind and rain and snow. The road by which we entered was the village's only link to the outside world. We saw no other vehicles. The villagers of Strinilas traveled on foot and by donkey on paths of dirt and ancient laid stone.

The bus dropped me off in front of the only *kafeneon* in the village, which was also the village's only store. I went inside, ordered a cup of Greek coffee, and sat at the corner table by the door. A constant stream of people flowed in and out of the shop to buy milk and bread and oth-er simple foods. I was sure I was seeing brother, sister, aunt, uncle, and cousin greeting one another. They exchanged very little money; rather, the *kafeneon* owner, a kind-looking man wearing a white apron, marked each transaction on a piece of paper, a debt to be paid later or to be worked out in barter.

The three other tables in the little *kafeneon* were occupied by old men wearing baggy pants and tattered, patched coats thrown cape-like over their shoulders. Their deeply wrinkled faces and cracked, arthritic fingers spoke of a life of both soil and toil. They sipped coffee, smoked unfil-tered cigarettes, and gossiped with a passion, as if their little mountain village were the capitol, and the fate of Greece, both ancient and mod-ern, hinged on their every word. Yet they were relaxed, almost playful in their passion, as if they knew that the mantle of their civilization had already passed to future generations, and that for all practical purposes they had already taken their place beside the Greeks of old.

I realized that at that very moment old Greek men were sitting in village *kafeneons* from the Albanian border to Turkey, from Bulgaria to Crete. They were meeting over innumerable tables with tiny cups of coffee balanced upon their knees. It was thus they greeted the day as they have, it would seem, since the very beginning of time. A tiny cup of coffee balanced on the knee of an old Greek man achieves a balance few of us can ever hope to achieve.

A deck of cards was on the table before me. I stared at it, took a deep breath, and said aloud, "Ace of spades." I cut the cards, turned my hand over to see what card I had picked, and there it was—sure enough—the ace of spades. I paid for my coffee and stepped out onto the street.

Chapter 5

The village of Strinilas moved with a rhythm of life deeply rooted both in the past and in the everyday. Children played in the street. As I walked past them, some ran to look at me while the more timid of them became frightened and ran to the shelter of their doorways or to hide behind their mothers' aprons. Then the mothers began calling the older children to come inside; it was time to change into their uniforms and go to school. Soon children were coming through their arched whitewashed doorways, their faces scrubbed almost to a polish and their hair, still wet, plastered to their heads. Their uniforms were crisp and blue as the sky. They carried books now under their arms. Once the kids were off to school their mothers could begin their daily chores. They went to the village wells with baskets of laundry and long ropes attached to buckets. There they met and talked and saw me, a stranger walking by.

I walked through the village, down the narrow, winding ways, past small courtyards bright with flowers. At the edge of the village, where the green patchwork of fields began, I watched the people work, plowing the earth and hoeing weeds. Beyond the fields the land dropped off so precipitously that all one could see beyond was the blue Adriatic, thousands of feet below. I sat with my back against a roadside shrine to the Virgin Mary that was lit by a small olive oil lamp. From this perspective the village was sharply contrasted against the dark, barren earth. The towering rock above the village dwarfed the achievements of people upon this rocky slope. The rich green valley that lay before me seemed only a tiny consolation for a life eked out of a barren, lifeless place.

Walking back to the village, hoping to notice an empty house, wondering how I would communicate my wish to rent it for the winter, wondering also whether the people of this village would take well to having a stranger living in their midst, I came upon an old and weathered sign. It was nailed to a wooden post that was leaning so heavily to the side that I thought the next gust of wind or even a pebble thrown by one of the village children would knock it down. The letters, which were worn, in the Greek alphabet. Though Greek lettering was still new to me, I was able to mouth out the sounds. It said Pantokrator. A barely discernible arrow on the sign pointed up a steep and narrow rocky road. Since this mountain had beguiled me for so long, and since the day was still young, I decided to follow the narrow road up the mountain. I wanted at least once to set foot on top of the highest mountain on Corfu. I longed to see the island laid out as on a map, to stand alone on top of the highest point and have an unobstructed view in all directions. Pantokrator is one of the Greek names for God. It means *all-powerful*.

The road mounted the slope above the village at an oblique angle. At the top of this slope, where I expected the land to rise again to the top of the mountain, a plateau opened out before me. Rocks jutted out at odd angles, new rocks, not yet worn by the passage of time. Their disordered array resembled ice on a river that had let loose then been dammed at a narrow passage. Rock lay upon rock, forming holes and tiny caves in the random array. Titanic forces had once broken to the surface here, and the rocks looked so freshly surfaced that I expected to hear them rumble beneath my feet. But this lunar landscape was pervaded by a profound silence. Not a bird sang, nor was there a tree to catch the gusting wind and turn its movement to song. This plateau seemed to be the very roof of the world.

At the far end of the plateau was the final cone of Pantokrator. It rose from the landscape as if some god had let rubble slide through his fingers, or some heavenly hourglass had let its sands run out. The road wound its way across the plateau to the cone's base; then it switched back and forth to the summit. And on the summit I now saw what looked like a fortress or a castle with high stone battlements.

About halfway across the plateau I heard a chicken clucking. Turning toward the noise, at first I saw nothing, just the same random array of rocks that surrounded me on all sides. Then a pattern arose out of the stones, much as a photograph appears in a tray of developer, and I realized there was a small farmhouse with outbuildings not more than twenty feet away. The buildings were made from the stone close at hand; the walls, which in places had caved in, blended in perfectly with their surroundings. Even more astounding than having a farm suddenly appear out of nothing was the realization that the presence of a chicken indicated that someone actually lived there. But why? The village of Strinilas was nestled in a fold of the mountain where there was warmth and security, water and terraced fields. Here was nothing but stone, the plateau, the deep descent of land and, across the sea and in the distance, the wild and ragged mountains of Albania.

Farther on I heard a faint tinkling of bells. The sound grew louder and softer as I followed the road up and down the small hills. Gradually the bells got louder until I saw goats jumping from boulder to boulder, searching out little bits of brush to eat. They jumped across the road before me and soon I was walking through a small flock of goats, the bells around their necks ringing gently. A goatherd stood in the shade of a huge boulder. He raised his staff and beckoned me. I was glad for the shade; the sun was now high in the sky. We sat on a stone. I pulled out my lunch and offered half to the herder. He accepted wordlessly.

The sun had darkened the goatherd's face; his hands were rough and callused. His clothes were old and tattered, patched and ripped again. His manner was rough. He seemed half-wild, un-tempered by the company of other men, his ways more in keeping with his four-legged companions with whom he roamed day after day. He tore large pieces from the loaf of bread and took handfuls of olives, spitting out the pits carelessly. We washed our food down with water from a flask the goatherd had slung over his shoulder. He gave me a cigarette. We didn't speak a word; we didn't even try. He knew I didn't speak his language, and I knew he didn't speak mine. For all I knew he could have been dumb. Replete, we sat in the cool shade and watched the goats in their endless scramble for food, their melodic bells ringing softly.

Leaving him to the companionship of his flock, I continued toward the cone of Pantokrator. At the base of the cone next to the road was an old, solidly built house nestled between the edge of the plateau and the steep land behind. Its shutters were locked, the front door padlocked shut. A small oasis, consisting of a few trees and small patches of grass surrounded the house. Some earlier inhabitants had leveled the slopes of the mountain to create a few terraced fields, which time had tried to efface: the rock walls that held the terraces up were crumbling and the little fields themselves were overrun with weeds and stunted trees. Yet the house itself looked tended. A bucket stood beside a stone-lined well. I drew some water and poured it over my head.

Above the house the road rose steeply through a series of switchbacks to the final summit of the mountain. In places the road was washed out; in others, stone and rubble had tumbled off the mountain and blocked the way. The elements were obviously in variance with this road; left to itself, in time, the zigzagging scar would be obliterated.

What would take longer to obliterate was the stone fortress on top of the mountain. As I mounted the final switchbacks its high stone wall towered over me, and I saw something move above the wall— perhaps a person clothed in black. The next time I looked, the black figure was gone.

Turning the last corner in the road, I came upon a closed metal gate in the high stone wall, above which was a bell tower. As I peered through the gate I realized that what I had thought was a fortress or a castle was actually a monastery. Stepping away from the gate, I stood on a boulder overhanging the steep back side of the mountain. Villages dotted the coast and Corfu Town shone in the distance. The wind rode the slope of the mountain and howled in my ears. I leaned into the wind not to get blown away.

The metal gate creaked behind me. Turning, I saw a black-robed monk. He had just come through the gate and he was securing it, his back turned toward me, his robe fluttering in the wind, causing his form to shift and change shape.

When he turned I saw that his long beard was mostly white, and though he was old he moved with agility. He gathered the ends of his robe in his hands and came toward me.

"*Yassas,*" I called out to him, hello.

He returned my greeting. Then he said something in Greek that I did not understand. So I recited one of the few sentences I knew in Greek.

"I do not speak Greek," I told him. It pained me to have to say this, to have come to this man's lonely mountaintop and not be able to speak his language.

He shrugged as if to say it didn't matter.

It was then that I noticed the monk's eyes. At first I thought they struck me because they were dark as coal yet shone with a light that seemed more than that reflected by the sun. But then I realized his eyes did not both look in the same direction. His left eye was fixed on me, his right eye directed somewhere over my left shoulder, as if he were seeing something hovering there. And his dominant eye switched. He fixed me first with one eye then the other. It was an odd feeling, as if he were seeing something just on the periphery.

He came up beside me and looked out over the vista that fell away below our feet. No words were necessary to take in such beauty. Silence suited the place well. It was a good place for a monastery. Modern civilization had too often crowded in on other monasteries in Greece, such as the one on Corfu's west coast, surrounded now by tourist beaches. This place was different.

Chapter 6

The monk turned to me, smiled, and asked if I wanted coffee. I said yes, and we walked through the ancient stone gate with ironwork doors and entered the monastery's courtyard.

A few stunted trees grew in the middle of the courtyard, on either side of which were long, low buildings built right into the monastery's stone wall. Along the length of the buildings were doors that led into separate cells. Each cell had a single window, crosshatched by iron bars. At the far end of the courtyard a set of stairs ascended to a smaller courtyard and the monastery's church. Obviously older than the other buildings, its walls were smooth and newly whitewashed and its roof was rounded in the Byzantine style. Higher than the other buildings, the church stood out sharply against the deep blue sky.

The monk's long robe played gracefully with the wind as I followed him across the courtyard. He led me into a simple, Spartan kitchen. A few pots and pans hung from nails driven into the whitewashed walls, and a large cupboard held cups and plates, bowls and silverware. A half-eaten loaf of bread lay upon a roughly hewn wooden table. Braided garlic hung from the ceiling. There was a two-burner gas stove, and over a stone sink was a single faucet. A window overlooking the courtyard provided the only light. He led me through the kitchen into a low-ceilinged room in which stood a long table with a bench on either side. He motioned for me to sit. Then he went back to the kitchen to brew coffee.

In the meantime, I took out my pocket English-Greek dictionary and worked out a few simple questions to ask him about his life on the mountain. I could tell by the way he had looked out over the mountains that his love for the mountains mirrored my own. I wanted to get to know this man.

Soon he returned with two small cups of Greek coffee and sat down across the table from me.

"How old are you?" I asked.

"Sixty-one."

"How many years have you lived here?"

"Forty."

"How many other people live here?"

"None."

I looked up the word *alone*.

"Alone?" I asked.

"Yes," he replied.

The process of speaking with him was laborious. He knew not a single word of English. But he had patience. Once, when I couldn't understand one of his answers, he pulled a pair of thick reading glasses out of his robe, squinted into the tiny dictionary, and looked up the word. Then he pointed out its English equivalent.

After we drained our tiny cups to the thick black grounds, he brought out a bottle of ouzo and two small glasses. He filled each glass half-full with the clear liquid, then we clinked our glasses together. As we sipped our ouzo I asked him more questions, and though it was difficult, neither of us flagged. As I spent more time with him it became clear that he had a different relation to time than most people: for him, it seemed, time was unlimited. He drew patience from a well that knew no bottom.

This is what I found out from him: his name was Evdókimos Koskinás, and he was born and raised in Strinilas where two of his brothers still lived. He had a sister in Athens. His parents were dead, buried in the village cemetery. When he first moved to the monastery another monk lived there, a man whom he referred to as his teacher. They lived ten years together on the mountain. Then the older monk died. Since then he'd lived there alone. He was both a *monohós* and a *papa,* a monk and a priest, the priest for Strinilas. He received money from the Greek

Orthodox Church, but it wasn't much. The condition of his robe and the simplicity of his kitchen attested to this. He relied on the help and goodwill of the villagers. The people of Strinilas were good people, he told me, and his life had been good.

The man was as singular as the mountain; in fact, they shared certain features—some superficial, such as the deep furrowing lines that crossed his brow, so reminiscent of the well-worn fissures carved into the mountain's twisted rocks, and others that ran deep, as if the deeper the foundation, the wider and broader both the mountain and the man. Yet there was nothing grave about him. The lines on his face were not the lines of worry; they were not written in stone. Nothing seemed hardened in him. He was fluid. More than anything, he was full of life.

Once, when I chose a word that rendered my question an absurdity, he laughed so hard that I too couldn't help but laugh. When I found the correct word and put the question to him again, a knitted-brow concentration came over him as he sought an answer so simple that even *I* could understand. His face, like a child's, reflected directly the emotion he felt. When he told me his parents were dead, I saw the pain he felt at the loss, and when he said the people of Strinilas were good people, I saw the pride he felt for them.

I asked how old the monastery was. He waved his hand with his fingers outstretched as if to say the monastery's age was beyond reckoning. Then he crooked a finger and told me to follow him. We went out through the kitchen and walked along the monastery wall beyond it. The wall, the outside of which dropped twenty or thirty feet before reaching the mountain's slope, was from where we stood only waist high. Stopping a moment and gazing at the road winding across the plateau before disappearing over its edge, I realized that it was from here I had seen the black figure, the monk I was now following.

He brought me to the church, which shone so brilliantly in the sun that at first my eyes were useless in the dim interior. I groped after the monk, our footfalls echoing hollowly. Shafts of light streamed in through high, slit-like windows, casting woven patterns of light upon the floor's cool stone slabs. The body of the church was empty, the arched ceiling painted with cracked and water-stained frescoes depicting scenes from the life of Christ. From the walls hung icons, old and yellowed. Upon the altar, elevated by a single step, stood metal racks for candles. At the center of the altar an old and finely made wooden stand held a large, leather-bound Bible. The monk lit some candles, muttering a prayer beneath his breath.

We went back outside and leaned against the low wall beyond the kitchen. Below us, the mountain twisted and fell to the sea. It was a powerful scene, on a scale so vast that a village nestled in a deep fold on the mountain's steep descent to the sea appeared but a passing thought in the life of the mountain, a mere blink of the eye. One day even this monastery, which had stood so long, would crumble and be gone, leaving not a trace behind.

There are times when the very context of our lives is wider than the everyday. There are places that make this wider context manifest. From this mountaintop monastery I felt a glimmer of something vast.

How many monks must have spent their lives contemplating the scene I was now seeing for the first time? I thought of the search for God these heights must have engendered in them.

Without really considering what I was doing, I looked up the words to ask the monk one very simple question: "Do you see God?"

I was young at the time. I still believed the answer to be within reach. I thought: If something underlies it all, if there is a unity behind the diversity, and if it is possible to comprehend and experience that unity, then surely there must be people who have experienced it. These people would no doubt be rare, and they would have come to their realization by extraordinary means. It was reasonable to believe that they would live far from the distractions of a bustling world. It was my search for that experience, I then knew, that had drawn me to this mountaintop and why I was standing in the wind with this old monk.

I had put the words together from my dictionary. *Blepes Theo? Blepes,* you see; *Theo,* God. Do you see God?

My question caught him off guard. He flashed me a look like lightning. Then he waved his hands in front of himself as if to fend the question off. I realized he was pretending he didn't understand. He was nervously eyeing me to see whether I saw through his charade. There was something playful behind his act, mischievous rather than deceitful. He was truly flustered.

I repeated the question, and again he pretended not to understand. I looked up the words again, and repeated each word distinctly.

He turned, looked steadily back over the mountains, and let silence speak for what no words could communicate.

Suddenly I felt like the imprudent young American that I was, intruding upon ground I had no right to intrude upon. It was enough that he had shared the silence and peace of his monastery with me. I had gone a step too far in asking after the fruit of his many years of solitude.

I knew it was time to go.

I began the painstaking process of telling the monk I had to leave, that I had to go back to the village of Strinilas to search for a place to live. Again I felt bad for the hoops I put him through simply to understand me. But he was patient. He stumbled along with me as I looked up each word and constructed disjointed sentences. When he suddenly understood what I was trying to tell him his face lit up, he tapped a finger to his temple, and his eyes glimmered. He had an idea.

"*Éla mázi mu,*" he said, come with me.

I followed him past the kitchen to the next door. He opened it and we entered a small cell. He made a gesture to encompass the room.

"You live here," he said.

I was sure I had misunderstood him. I tapped my chest. "*I,*" I said. Then I held my open palm to the side of my head and inclined my head as if in sleep.

"Yes," he said, "yes, yes. You live here!"

He was speaking rapidly now. Greek flew over my head as my legs almost buckled beneath me. I could hear my heart pounding as if I were riding the crest of a wave, the wave of certainty that had driven me up the mountain. So this is it, I said to myself: I didn't even have to ask for it.

He stepped aside so I could examine the room.

The room was about twelve foot square and sparsely furnished. To the left of the door stood a bed made of roughly cut wooden planks on which a thin foam mattress lay. Above the bed, the room's only window looked out over the courtyard. Running almost the entire length of the room along the back wall was a long table and bench. A chair stood at the table's head. The room's whitewashed walls were rough, as was the ceiling, which was quite low. I stumbled back out into the courtyard, my mind stunned by his offer, my eyes smarting from the sun.

The monk followed me. He could wait no longer. "You like?" he asked.

"Yes," I said. "I like. Much I like."

"*Éla mázi mu,*" he said again, come with me. So I followed him into the kitchen. He picked up a box of matches, pretended to light a match, and pretended to light the gas burner. Then he put a big frying pan over the imagined flame. He diced some imaginary vegetables then tested the pan to make sure it was hot. He put the cut vegetables into the pan, stirred them with an imaginary spoon, then divided them between two imaginary plates. He then pretended to eat. All the while he hummed softly to himself, absorbed in his culinary arts. He was showing me we could eat there together, and it was a great performance. I clapped. He took a bow. We both laughed.

Then he showed me the outhouse. It was perched so precariously over the steep abyss that the hole in the floor seemed to open to eternity.

We crossed the courtyard. I was overwhelmed. My mind was swimming. He stopped and waited till I was fully facing him. He fixed me with his left eye. His right eye was looking over my shoulder, as if something was hovering there.

He asked, "You live here?"

"Yes," I said.

He clapped me forcefully on the shoulder with his open palm. "Good," he said. "Good!" He told me I could move in any time. I told him I'd return within the week.

He saw me to the gate and told me to wait. He rushed to the kitchen and returned a moment later with a handful of shelled almonds. I filled my shirt pocket.

When the monk was out of sight I ran to an outcropping on the side of the mountain and let out the joyous shout that I'd been holding back since he'd first opened the door to the cell and said, "You live here." I jumped from boulder to boulder then ran back to the road.

Stopping at the house by the unkempt terraced fields, I looked up and saw him leaning over the wall at the mountain's summit. I waved my arms over my head, and he returned my farewell.

Chapter 7

By the time I was walking up the path to the house in Kontókali it was late afternoon. Andy and Ann were sitting on the front step, and when I reached them Andy said, "You'll never guess what happened to us today. Even when we tell you, you won't believe it."

"You won't believe what happened to *me*," I said. "Let me tell you first." So I told them how I had gone up the mountain, met the monk, and been invited to live there with him. They became as excited as I was over the events of my day. We made coffee, reestablished our perch on the front step, and Andy recounted his own story that seemed even more unbelievable than mine.

First he described the beginning of a typical, lazy day in Kontókali. They had slept late, eaten fresh figs smeared on toast, done a bit of laundry in the stone basin behind the house, then eaten lunch. After lunch they decided to take a walk. Calling their cat—who always enjoyed going on walks—they were about to leave when they heard voices in the olive grove.

It was Giorgos, and he was not alone. This time he wasn't with his jockey-sized roofer. Nor was he with the policemen. This time coming up the path with Giorgos was an army general in full military regalia. Behind them were two soldiers, each shouldering an end of the same old wooden ladder.

The general greeted Andy and Ann in English, which they took as a bad sign. What did an English-speaking general want with *them?* They felt better when the general showed himself to be a jovial sort and told them he had learned English when he was in the United States visiting his brother who owned a pizza shop somewhere in New Jersey. They talked a while about pizza, New Jersey, and the United States while Giorgos instructed the soldiers where to put the ladder. When it was in place the general excused himself. First Giorgos climbed the ladder and peered into the hole. He came down and muttered something to the general. Then the general climbed the ladder, peered into the hole, came down, and muttered something to the soldiers.

Unable to stomach the endless repetition of this strange ritual, Andy and Ann went back inside. But after almost half an hour, Andy began to wonder what was taking them so long. So he stepped out the back door just in time to see the general backing down the ladder, cradling in his arms an old and rusted metal cylinder. When the general reached the ground, he yelled out, "Hey, buddy! You better look out. I have a *bomb!*"

"*Right*," Andy said, and hurried back inside. When Andy told Ann what the general had told him, Ann convinced him he had misunderstood. A bomb—now *that* was absurd.

After another twenty minutes they decided to take that walk. They called the cat again and went out the front door. But as they rounded the corner of the house they heard a gunshot followed by an enormous explosion. The concussive wave that followed almost swept them off their feet. The cat screeched and shot off down the hill. (It still hadn't returned while they were telling me the story.) Andy and Ann hid behind the corner of the house shaking with fear. When they poked their heads around the corner they saw a mushroom-shaped cloud of smoke rising from the olive grove. Giorgos, the general, and the soldiers soon appeared, jauntily walking back toward the house, their faces flushed with triumph.

Giorgos explained to them what had happened: During World War II the Italians occupied Corfu. The Corfiots resisted in whatever way they could, though being an unarmed civilian population there wasn't much they could do. The Italians camped everywhere and caused trouble wherever they went. Some camped in the olive grove in front of the house. Giorgos' uncle couldn't help but notice that the troops in front of his family's house were guarding a stockpile of bombs. So he did what any resourceful person would do under the circumstances: one night, after the troops had drunk themselves into oblivion, he stole one of the bombs and hid it in the roof. He then waited for an opportunity to use it on the foreign aggressors. But alas, the opportunity never arose. The Italians withdrew, and the memory of the bomb died with the uncle some years later, leaving behind a family legend that no one really believed. That is, until the jockey-sized roofer removed the tiles to examine the condition of the beams and discovered it.

This explained so much. It explained why Giorgos had been so adamant that Andy and Ann vacate the room. It explained why the police had come, then the army general. And it explained why the roof's condition was such a concern to all of them. The only thing it didn't explain was why Giorgos hadn't warned us sooner.

Giorgos explained: "I didn't want to scare you."

It was one hell of a crazy day.

While I prepared dinner, Andy and Ann walked to the village to buy cigarettes. When I heard them coming up the path I grabbed a lantern and greeted them at the door.

"Perfect timing!" I yelled into the darkness. "Dinner is ready."

Ann said, "Hold your horses, it can wait, you'd better sit down."

I sat.

"I'm going to London!" Ann blurted out.

"You're *what?*" I said.

"I'm London bound. I'm going on Monday. There was a guy hanging out at the kiosk, looking for someone to buy the return half of his airplane ticket. He came from London on a two-week holiday, met a woman on a sailboat, and now he is sailing off with her to Crete. He was desperate to sell it. He only wanted the equivalent of twenty dollars. It was an offer we couldn't refuse. We've been planning to go for Christmas anyway, to visit my mother and get more of our stuff. We won't stay as long as Christmas, but this way we can both fly."

"Both?" I said.

"Yes," Andy said. "It's so cheap that now I can get a normal flight—and we'll *still* be saving money."

"There is only one hitch," Ann said tentatively.

"Yes," Andy said, "there's just one favor…"

"Well," I said, "what is it?"

"We need someone to watch over the place and feed the cat."

"*Óxi problema*," I said. "No problem. The monastery's been on the mountain for over half a millennium. It'll be there. I can wait."

After dinner we decided to go to bed early before anything else could happen.

The next few days went off without a hitch. Andy secured a seat on a plane to London the following Saturday; it wasn't as soon as he would have liked, but it would do. I went up the mountain to tell the monk I'd be delayed a few weeks. Luckily, I stopped off at the *kafeneon* in Strinilas. The owner guessed correctly that I was the "*filos tu papa*," the friend of the priest. News of my coming had spread. He told me the monk was in Corfu Town for his monthly meeting with all the other priests and monks on the island. He promised to give my message to him when he returned.

Chapter 8

It was Monday morning. I half awoke from deep sleep to see Andy help Ann with her bag. They went out the door and into the early dawn. Andy was walking Ann to the village where Ann would catch a bus town. She was on her way to London. Her flight was at nine o'clock, but she had to get there early. Once they left, I fell easily back to sleep.

I stirred again when I heard Andy come in and go back to his bedroom. The sky was brighter now—pink and red. I heard roosters in the distance. I drifted back to sleep again.

I awoke with a start. Someone was pounding on the door. Pulling on my clothes, I stumbled into the main room; Andy came out of his room as well, sleep still in his eyes. Together we opened the door.

It was Giorgos. He was saying something about the police. They had just come to his house looking for Andy, and though we couldn't get his story straight, it sounded serious. "Oh, Ann," Andy muttered beneath his breath, "where are you when we need you to interpret?"

Then it occurred to us that maybe something had happened to Ann. We tried to get more details from Giorgos, but we gave up. Thanking Giorgos, we reassured him that Andy would go to the police station in town. I made coffee while Andy washed, shaved, and put on clean clothes: he had to look presentable for the police.

We caught the bus to town, and while Andy went to the police station I went to the Chess Café to wait for him.

About an hour later I was sitting at our usual table, a game of chess set up before me, when Andy walked in, his face deadly pale. Slouching in the chair opposite me, he reached out his hand, lifted the king, and laid it on its side.

"The game's over," he said.

"What do you mean?"

"Just that," he said. "I'm being kicked out of the country."

"*What?*"

"Remember the last form, the one that still had to be approved, the one that had to go to Athens?"

"Yeah—what about it?"

"You know the one," Andy continued as if he hadn't heard me, "the residence permit, the one we were going for in the *first* place, the one that we were trying to *get* by starting a business? The Main Man explained to me that a residence permit must gain approval from many government agencies in Athens before it's issued, one of which is the secret police. That's where mine caught a snag. My permit has been rejected by the secret police! But it wasn't only rejected—it's not as simple as that—that would have been too easy! They sent word to the Main Man to kick me out of the country.

"'You must go, you must leave Corfu,' he said.

"I asked him why the secret police wanted me out. He said he didn't know, or he couldn't tell me—I couldn't tell which he meant. The *secret police!* Apparently, they don't have to give a reason. That's why they're called the *secret* police. They do as they like. *They* answer no questions. They're like the CIA, but even more sleazy, more secretive. They're probably a holdover from the days of the colonels. Everybody is afraid of them. Even the Main Man. I could tell. It was strange, but he was treating me as if I were a security threat, as if I posed some kind of danger to the welfare of the country!

"But—" I said, unable to complete my sentence. "This is madness! Did he say when you have to go?"

Andy sighed. "He sure did, and here's how he decided: in a haphazard way, as if he were daydreaming, he flipped through his calendar and stopped at the page for Thursday. He pointed at it. I told him I already had a reservation on a plane for London on Saturday. But he said, 'No. You must go. You must leave Corfu—here,' and he pointed again to Thursday."

A wave of indignation swept over me, a flood of moral outrage. "They can't just kick you out like that," I said. "What about the business, the time you've invested, all the forms, the stamps of approval, and the money you've sunk into it, all those lawyer's fees? Think of the loom— and don't forget the wool; maybe it's even waiting for you in Ioánnina. They can't *do* that."

But of course they could. What I said was absurd, wasted energy. Secret police dwell beyond the moral sphere.

Andy ordered a cup of coffee. We sat in silence till it arrived, staring dumbly at the old men slapping cards on the other tables. I could tell by the look on his face that Andy was asking himself if this might be the last time he would see the players' antics, if we had already played our last game of chess in the Chess Café.

When Andy's coffee arrived I told him we'd have to fight it.

"I know," he said. "But how? The worst part is that Ann isn't here. When I arrived at the police station, I had to wait for the Main Man to see me. I was standing on a balcony on the station's second floor. I looked at my watch. It was exactly nine o'clock. Then I heard the plane, *her* plane, taking off from the airport. It flew right over the police station. If Ann had been looking out the window, we could have waved to each other. An instant later the Main Man called me into his office. He sat me down. And then, with no preliminary, he said, 'You must leave Corfu.' His timing was impeccable. I think he planned it that way."

A look of despair crossed Andy's face. "God," he said. "Maybe— behind the smiling and helpful front he presented to us every morning during all those months—the Main Man knew that this would be the final outcome. Maybe he woke up this morning with a smile on his face, knowing today was the big day." Andy sighed again. "I can tell you this," he said, "we have a battle ahead of us."

During the days that followed we spent most of our waking hours at the telephone exchange inside adjacent wooden booths dialing, dialing, and dialing, getting busy signals and then dialing again. Telephoning off the island of Corfu was a horrendous task. There couldn't have been more than a single line laid under the sea to the mainland. It was like playing the lottery—or Russian roulette—but instead of our fingers pulling a trigger, our trigger finger went the rounds of the rotary dial, hoping for a happy outcome. I dialed the same number so many times that I feared the number would be etched in my memory forever. I feared the harsh and annoying busy signal would haunt my dreams till my dying day.

Our first call was to the American Embassy in Athens. When we finally got through, Andy described the situation to one of the attachés, who agreed to investigate. He told Andy to call back later that day.

Next we went to Andy's lawyer to see if there was any legal recourse. The lawyer said there probably wasn't. He offered to call the Main Man for the details of the ruling. The biggest hope he could offer was that *perhaps* we could appeal.

Back at the telephone exchange we attempted to call Ann in London. It took us almost three hours to get through to her. Andy told her the bad news. He filled her in on all the sordid details. He told her we'd call the next day.

A quick trip back to the lawyer offered no great hope. The Main Man, the lawyer informed us, was merely acting on orders given by the secret police, and their rulings were usually as incontestable as they were secret. The lawyer tried to get Andy to confess to the crime that the secret police must have uncovered. The lawyer told us that if he knew the offense, then perhaps he could help. But without as much as a single unpaid parking ticket to blight his record, Andy hadn't a thing to confess. This only raised the lawyer's suspicions.

Back at the telephone exchange, our fingers were becoming stiff from dialing. When Andy got through to the embassy, the attaché said he was still looking into the matter, and that Andy should call back the next morning. With this, Andy became upset. He told the attaché he didn't have too many mornings left; he reminded him again of the Thursday deadline and implored him to work quickly. The attaché said he understood and hung up.

We left the telephone exchange totally exhausted and wandered aimlessly through the streets and back alleyways of Corfu until we passed a small taverna with wisps of delicious-smelling smoke wafting from its open doorway. Unable to resist the temptation, I tugged on Andy's sleeve and we veered inside.

We followed our noses to the kitchen, pointed out what we wanted from large, steaming pots on the stove, ordered beer, and sat down at a table near the front of the taverna. We drank our beer slowly, staring out the restaurant's open door.

Directly across the narrow street was a vegetable shop, next to which was a small shop that sold hardware. It was late in the day and business was slow. The two shop owners had pulled their stools onto the sidewalk. They sat talking to each other and smoking cigarettes as they probably had every evening for the last half century.

A boy no more than five years old came running up the street, chasing a puppy. First he and the puppy passed us from right to left; a moment later the puppy came running by again, the boy close behind. Then the boy and the puppy caught the attention of the shop owners across the street, and we could see them laughing at something just out of our view. Soon we saw what they were laughing at: the boy and puppy came back, but this time the boy was first and the puppy was nipping at his heels. The poor kid looked terrified, the puppy triumphant. We were still laughing over this scene when we saw the boy's angry mother march by with the puppy under one arm and the boy under the other.

The moment they were out of view an old woman appeared, leading a donkey over laden with burlap sacks. Then a man on a bicycle appeared, holding a large bag crooked in his arm. He swerved around an old man walking with the aid of a cane, startled the donkey, and the donkey dropped its load. The bicyclist stopped, the old woman yelled, and the old man, oblivious to everything, hobbled away. The woman and the bicyclist started arguing.

Then a policeman ambled up the road and the woman accosted him, telling the whole story with her arms. She pantomimed the story so clearly that even though we couldn't hear we knew exactly what she was saying. Then the bicyclist gave his side of the story, pointing this way and that, and the two began arguing again.

Meanwhile a crowd had gathered and the donkey still stood with the bags on the ground around it. The donkey was the only one who didn't mind the situation. One of the sacks he had been carrying was full of fresh greens. He fiddled it open with his thick lips and was enjoying a hearty meal. Then the two shop owners got into the fray. They pointed at the donkey and the sacks lying on the road. Then the shop owners, the bicyclist, and the policeman loaded the sacks onto the donkey, and the old woman led the donkey away. The crowd dispersed. The shop owners sat down again, lit cigarettes, and this little slice of life on Corfu went on as if nothing had happened.

When our meal came, Andy and I spoke of what a wonderful documentary film one might make depicting life on Corfu by simply mounting a camera in this (or any other) taverna and letting the film role. It was our only moment of respite in an otherwise difficult day.

Chapter 9

Next morning we headed straight for the telephone exchange and hammered away in our separate booths until we got through to the embassy in Athens. The attaché told Andy he had spoken to one of the officials at the secret police, who would only confirm the ruling in the case. He further speculated that, since Andy's background was clean, the decision to kick him out of the country was probably political.

The general election in Greece was only a few months away, and it looked as if PASOK, the socialist party, would gain control of the country. Since PASOK was anti-American, the attaché theorized that the official at the secret police responsible for issuing the order to deport Andy had probably wanted to secure his position under the new regime by having it on his record that he had kicked out an American. The attaché ended the conversation abruptly by stating that the embassy never interfered in Greek internal affairs.

We walked outside. Andy said, "It feels as if the noose is tightening. I think it's time we call in the reinforcements. We've got to pull out our trump card."

"What do you mean?" I asked.

Andy told me that Jordan, a close friend of the family, had been working with the Greek government, promoting American businesses in Greece. Jordan had told Andy that if he ever ran into trouble, he should call him. "I think it is time to make that call," Andy said.

We decided the best way to contact Jordan was to have Ann call him first from London, where calls go through in a single dialing. When we finally got through to her, Ann told Andy she'd call him. Andy said to Ann that we'd call her back in a few hours.

In the mean time, we did some shopping and checked our mail at the post office. Andy received a note from the wool dyer in Ioánnina, which we had translated. The wool was ready and waiting in Igumenitsa, the port on the mainland about half an hour's boat ride from Corfu. How incredibly ironic—just in time for Andy to be kicked out of the country.

We went to the port and studied the ferryboat schedule to Igumenitsa. We decided that Andy had just enough time to take the ferry to the mainland to get the wool before we had to call Ann. So he set off for the mainland as I went to Kontókali to put the food away and feed the cat. Andy arrived home with five big sacks of wool whose fate was as uncertain as his own. We rushed back to town to launch our next offensive at the telephone exchange, which was beginning to feel more like home than our quiet abode in the olive grove.

This time the telephone exchange was busy; we had to wait a long time just to get a booth. As Andy dialed, I talked to a Frenchman who had been trying to call Paris for three days. I believed him. His disheveled clothes and stubble beard attested to his struggle. Somehow, quite miraculously—and to the great distress of the Frenchman—Andy got through to London in less than half an hour. Ann told him she had talked to Jordan. She had the name and number of a high official in the embassy in Athens whom, Jordan had said, he would have briefed by the time we could get through to him. So we dialed Athens.

The official that Andy contacted said he would try to use his influence on the secret police and that we should sit tight. He told Andy not to worry about the Thursday deadline. Nobody, he said, would bother him if he stayed a few extra days.

So the war went on. We were in the trenches now, fighting the final campaign. We had called in the reinforcements and the special diplomatic teams. We made another trip to the lawyer to update him on recent developments. He agreed with the official at the embassy that Andy could stretch the Thursday deadline by a few days, but Andy was leery. It was fine that the embassy and his lawyer said he could stretch it, but what about the Main Man, the one who would come to get him? He might not agree. We went home. Andy packed. He left his bag by the back door just in case.

The next day was Thursday, Andy's deadline. We woke early and took the bus to town. Everywhere eyes seemed to follow us. At the edge of town, a man dressed in a dark business suit got on the bus. Business suits were rare on Corfu. He sat directly across from us and stared. He was holding a hat under his arm; then he put it on. It was a policeman's hat. Our hearts were pounding. The bus stopped at a light, and when the light turned green, Andy jumped from the bus.

We met at the telephone exchange. Jordan's mysterious friend at the embassy said he was unable to influence the decision handed down by the secret police. He said he was sorry, but there was nothing more he could do.

That was it. We had pulled our last string and it had failed. We went to a travel agent and changed Andy's reservation to the next day, Friday. Then we dialed London to tell Ann the bad news.

Ann had talked to Jordan again. He had one other friend in the Greek government who could possibly help us. Jordan said his friend was already 'working on it.' Ann gave us the man's number, though Jordan had refused to give the man's name. So we called our last hope in Athens.

If Jordan's friend at the embassy had sounded like a spy, this man, according to Andy, sounded like the spy chief. His muffled voice seldom rose above a whisper, yet it echoed, as if off the concrete walls of an underground bunker. He had few words and his manner was curt. He told Andy that he was investigating the case and that Andy should call back at five past three that afternoon.

So we wandered around town. Andy said good-bye to friends. At three we started dialing, and miraculously at exactly five past we got through to Jordan's friend in the Greek government in Athens. He said there was nothing he could do. Andy told him the Embassy's theory about the upcoming election, but the man in the Greek government dismissed it. "If that were the only reason," he said, "I would certainly have been able to intervene. But they have certain *information*." He would say no more.

Now the game really *was* over. We had called all the resources at our disposal, to no avail. Even the mysterious high official—the man we imagined speaking from the underground bunker—could do nothing. Later, we found out that he was Greece's finance minister.

I went home and Andy went to the police station to tell the Main Man he need not come to get him since he would be leaving the next day on his own volition. When Andy returned he told me the Main Man was apologetic to him. He also offered some friendly advice: he told Andy that if he stayed out of the country for a week or two he could return on a regular tourist visa. Athens would never know, and although he couldn't work, he could spend another three months on Corfu. Andy decided he would see how Ann felt about returning. In a few days, they would send me a telegram from London.

Friday was a black day. We were exhausted from the fight. Now that it was over we felt deflated. I helped Andy down the hill with his luggage. We rode the bus to town in silence, and after a few words of farewell he was gone.

With a lump in my throat, I wandered aimlessly around the winding alleys of Corfu Town. At the port, I watched an old man sitting on a crate, fishing. Waves lapped gently against the landing. Across the bay, the mountain Pantokrator rose in its solitary gray silence.

Back in Kontókali, it felt strange being alone in the house. I lit a lantern and cooked a meal. The cat came in and I gave her some of the tiny fish that she loved. I kept reminding myself that Andy and Ann might very well be coming back in a week or so. Now I just had to wait for their telegram.

Later that evening I sat at the table to read by the light of a lantern when the cat jumped inside through an open window and ran beneath the table. I started playing with her, rolling her around with my bare feet, when

I realized she wasn't really playing with me. Something cool moved across my skin and slithered between my toes. I lifted the lantern, brought it low beside me, and leaned over. A shriek spontaneously burst from my lips as I fell backwards, my chair splintering beneath me. My cry and the sound of splintering wood startled the cat, but she continued to claw at the beast that was desperately trying to free itself from her grip: a small green snake.

I took a leg of what was once my chair and brought it down with accuracy on the snake's head, killing it instantly. I fell back on the floor, gasping for breath. What was it someone had once told me about snakes on Corfu? Wasn't it the small ones, the ones no bigger than a pencil, that were deadly poisonous?

I wrapped the snake in a piece of newspaper so I could show it to someone the next morning. In the mean time, I tried to be calm and rational. I told myself that I had never seen a snake in the house before. I probably never would again. But my sleep was disturbed that night by dreams so vivid that I awoke many times unsure whether the snakes I saw crawling across the floor were real or imagined.

Next morning I took the snake in the crumpled piece of newspaper down the path to the pig farm. The farmer's wife was out feeding the chickens. When I approached her and unfolded the paper, she jumped back, gasped, and shrieked, "*Estreetas!*"

This brought her husband running from the barn. As the farmer's wife pointed to the mangled snake, the farmer put his hand to his forehead and exclaimed, "*Po, po, po,*" as if he were going to faint. He asked where I had found it. I pointed up the hill and said *spiti moo*, my house. "Inside?" he asked. I nodded.

His wife shook her head. "*Kako, kako, kako,*" she said, bad, bad, bad. Her husband joined in. They both stood there shaking their heads, saying, "Bad, bad, bad!" Then the farmer made a motion like a snake striking, and he said, "One hour and—KAPUT!"

I continued down the hill to the village. I had to investigate. I had to find out how the villagers kept snakes away from their houses, and what they did if bitten. Until I knew all there was to know, I couldn't sleep in that house again.

First I went to Demetrios, the man who ran the taverna where I had stayed during my first trip to Corfu. He spoke English fluently and had a good head on his shoulders. He was a real solid citizen. I was hoping he'd tell me that the people at the pig farm had exaggerated, that there were no snakes on Corfu that could dispatch one with such haste. But when I told him that the farmer's wife at the pig farm had yelled *estreetas*, he winced. He translated the word for me: viper. He said one's only hope when bitten by one of these snakes was to get to the hospital for an anti-venom injection within one hour. Otherwise, that hour would be your last. It would also be your most painful.

He told me a couple of stories about snakes in general and vipers in particular. They were horrible stories, enough to make my blood run cold. He told me that snakes are attracted to milk. When he was a young boy, a woman in the village was working in a field with her infant child. She breast fed him and left him on a blanket at the field's edge. A while later she returned to see a snake slithering down the sleeping baby's throat, following the scent of milk.

After a while I implored Demetrios to stop. "OK, you've convinced me," I said. "These snakes are a menace, they kill children, little babies barely out of their mother's wombs, but surely there is something one can do to keep them away."

"You're right," Demetrios replied. "The women burn something at the beginning of snake season every year. I'm not sure what they burn. It's women's duty. Let's go ask my mother."

So we went across the road to the village well where we found Demetrios' mother along with other village women. They were drawing water in buckets to wash clothes. Demetrios spoke to the women in Greek, explaining what had happened to me the night before. They listened to him, their mouths gaping. Then they crossed themselves and gasped. Pushing past Demetrios, they surrounded me, shaking their open hands toward the heavens. They spoke to me all at once. Obviously, I was in deep trouble.

Demetrios tried to interrupt them so he could translate, but had to speak above their clamor: "They say you should never kill the first snake you find in your house. You should show it out the door with kind words and a gentle request never to return. If you kill the first snake, all the other snakes will know it, and you'll never be rid of them. You have to make peace with the snake world, that's what they're saying; make violence toward snakes and that violence will be returned."

"Ask them," I implored, "what they burn to keep them away." Demetrios asked them, and then he translated. "They say you must burn leather shoes, old leather shoes, shoes that have been worn for years and have been run right to the ground. The smellier and more filled with holes the better." As he told me this, the women nodded their heads in agreement and pointed at their feet.

I thanked Demetrios and the women and proceeded to take the bus to town in search of old leather shoes. My first stop was the shop of Giorgos the sandal maker. Although Giorgos' shop was no larger than a closet, he produced the finest sandals on the island. He was both a local legend and, because he was a favorite among foreign visitors to the island, a character of international renown. He was known for drinking ouzo as if it were water.

I walked into his shop and found him sitting on a stool surrounded by huge piles of leather and tangled balls of leather chord. Before I could say *yassas*, he stood and informed me that he would buy me an ouzo. Giorgos the sandal maker transacted no business without first drinking with his customers. We crossed the street to a *kafeneon,* stood at the counter, and chugged the contents of our glasses in a single slug. Back at the shop, he sat down amid the piles of leather and asked what he could do for me.

Recounting the events of the previous evening, I told him the advice of the village women. I ended with a plea for old leather shoes. But I could tell what I said bothered him. "Those women no right," he said. "Burn old shoes, yes. But leather ones—NO!" He was roaring now. "Not leather shoes. *Plastic* shoes. You must burn old plastic shoes!"

"Giorgos," I said, "what you mean is that I must burn plastic. Plastic shoes, old plastic shoes—that can't matter. Plastic is plastic: it never changes. For thousands of years it remains plastic; it doesn't break down. It isn't biodegradable!" If I hadn't lost Giorgos before, I certainly did on the word *biodegradable*. Giorgos repeated his words as if they were a firm religious conviction written on a tablet of stone: "Burn old *plastic* shoe, snake go away."

I asked him if he had any old plastic shoes he didn't need. "No!" he boomed, bringing his fist down on his workbench. I had really insulted him now. Asking a leather craftsman for plastic shoes—an unforgivable blasphemy. I asked him for some leather scraps just in case they *did* work against snakes. He grudgingly gave me a few handfuls, which I stuffed into my pockets.

Slinking down back alleys, down market streets, and behind buildings, I looked in dumpsters, trash cans, and gutters for old, worn out, and discarded shoes. I searched for leather shoes, plastic shoes—it mattered little to me. The more people I asked what material to burn to drive away snakes, the further I would be drawing myself into folklore, a fascinating study in itself, but not my present and immediate aim, which was to drive away snakes. Since I had broken the cardinal rule—namely killing the first snake found in the house—the mixture I burned would have to be particularly noxious. I found a surprising number of old shoes, both leather and plastic, and I rounded off my collection with miscellaneous bits of plastic and paper. Then I returned to Kontókali.

As I walked along the path to the house I shied away from low branches and bushes. Surveying each step for lurking danger, I was held in sway by that dark corner of the mind that harbors an instinctual fear of snakes.

We burned our trash in an old olive oil tin we left in the high grass behind the house. When I lifted it I stood transfixed, staring at the spot where the tin had been. There, coiled in a perfect spiral, was another green snake. The snake lifted its head slowly, as if I had awakened it from an age-long slumber, flashed its tongue at me twice, and lazily slithered off into the grass. I stared at the flattened, matted grass where it had been sleeping, and I realized I could no longer stay there. The snakes had won.

I packed enough clothes and books for a long stay in town and left. I checked into the Cyprus Hotel. There, at least, I could go barefoot without the least concern of getting mortally wounded by a snake.

Chapter 10

Andy and Ann's promised telegram arrived the next day. It said they would arrive on Corfu the following Monday. This meant I had to spend another week at the Cyprus Hotel. Once they arrived, I would go to live on the mountain.

On Tuesday and Thursday of the following week I went briefly to the house in Kontókali to feed the cat. On Sunday, the day before their return, I mustered enough courage to burn the anti-snake mixture. Bringing the smoking olive oil tin inside the house, I let it smolder a few minutes in each room. By the end I had a horrendous headache.

Just when I was ready to leave, I heard someone call my name. It was our landlord Giorgos, and the moment I saw the look on his face I knew there was trouble. He was speaking quickly. It was difficult for me to understand him. But then he said *astinomía,* the word for police. That word I knew. He insisted I follow him to his house in the village.

Giorgos brought me inside his house and through the kitchen, where his wife was preparing Sunday dinner. He sat me on a straight-back wooden chair on a step outside the back door, and there he left me—alone, on the threshold, like a stray dog. If I leaned forward on the chair, I could watch Giorgos' wife tending to the steaming caldrons and pans of roasting meats. The smells that wafted from that kitchen were fantastic. They drove me mad with hunger.

Guests started arriving—Giorgos' parents, grown children, grandchildren, uncles, aunts, and cousins. Each one shot me a furtive glance when they came in to kiss the cook hello, and I could tell none of them knew why I was sitting alone on a chair just outside the kitchen door. And indeed I must have looked as forlorn and unsure as I felt. The police would arrive at any moment. I just wanted to get it over with.

Giorgos' daughter spoke English. When she arrived, I implored her to ask her father what the police wanted with me. When she returned from the kitchen, she said simply that earlier that morning a policeman had come to the house looking for me. I sked her why, but she didn't know. Or maybe she didn't want to say. She did tell me the police would be back soon.

Then Giorgos came out with an ancient uncle, a relic of an earlier age with a wild shock of gray hair and a huge waxed mustache. Giorgos placed a chair next to mine, helped his uncle sit in it, and handed each of us a glass. Then he got a bottle of ouzo, filled our glasses, put the bottle on the floor between us, and left us to our own resources. The old man cracked a smile, lifted his glass, and said, "To life!" "To life," I said, and gulped the ouzo down. The old man poured us each another glass.

When it came time for the feast, Giorgos' wife insisted that Giorgos couldn't just leave me alone by the door. Since they didn't know what else to do with me, they invited me to partake in their feast.

The dining room table was sumptuously decked out. There was a entire leg of lamb on a huge wooden board, a platter of fish, lasagna, salad, spinach and cheese pies, and a host of other dishes I couldn't begin to name. The smell of the roasted meat made my mouth water; the juices in my stomach flowed in happy anticipation. I could not believe my good fortune. To top this, Giorgos showed me to the seat of honor at the head of the table. The plates and silverware were so fine and old and delicate that they looked as if they were part of the dowry of someone who had died before Giorgos' grandparents were even born. Giorgos loaded my plate with food and set it before me. He filled my glass with a powerful homemade wine he had opened especially for the occasion. He made me drain my glass as he watched, then filled it again to the brim. I had the distinct feeling that he was trying to get my wheels nicely loosened for my approaching encounter with the police.

Giorgos piled more and more food onto my plate, as if he were fattening me for slaughter. Every time my glass was half-empty, he filled it again, as the ancient uncle, with whom I had drunk ouzo, looked at me now with an expression sympathetic to my impending doom. Even Giorgos' youngest grandson, who was only a toddler, pretended to pout whenever he looked my way. They all seemed to say, gazing with sudden, sullen looks: It's too bad what's about to happen to you, but who among us can change fate? I had one eye on the front window, waiting to see the police car pull in.

A car finally did arrive, but it was like no police car I had ever seen. Giorgos stood up, motioned for me to follow, and we went out to meet my fate. The police car was an unmarked black Mercedes Benz and the police man was a middle-aged man whose close-cropped hair was graying at the temples and whose dark suit and dark glasses made him look every bit the part of an agent of the secret police.

In perfect English, the policeman asked me what I was doing on Corfu. Then he got down to business. He wanted to know whether Andy and Ann were planning to come back to the island. I couldn't lie to him. I told him they were due to arrive the next day. He said, "When they come, they may stay two days, maybe three. They can pick up their belongings—but then they must go. They must leave Corfu! They must leave Corfu, and they must never return! Is this clear?"

"Y-yes," I stammered.

"You will give them a message?"

"Yes, I will."

"Tell them: two days, maybe three. But then they must leave. They must leave Corfu and they must never return!"

With that he got back into in his black Mercedes Benz and sped off.

Giorgos managed a weak smile. Muttering something about how sorry he was, he led me back to my place of honor at the head of the table. Filling my own glass now with the powerful homemade wine, I finished off the business Giorgos had begun. And while I could still lift myself from the table, I thanked my hosts and wound my way back up the hill to the house.

❧   ❧

After sleeping off the effects of Giorgos' wine at the house in Kontókali (snakes, at that moment, were not on my mind), I closed up the house and returned to my room at the Cyprus. I slept again and awoke when it was dark. Then, wanting to take along books to read while on the mountain, I went to the library at the Anglican Church, which was only open on Sunday evenings and was as much a social club as a library.

I had tea and homemade cookies, and was checking my books out before leaving when the elderly British woman who acted as librarian insisted I go and introduce myself to the new vicar. The vicar was regaling a group of people with stories at the far corner of the room.

Because the congregation of the Anglican Church of Corfu was not large enough to support a full-time vicar, one was sent each month from England. The vicar—and his family if he had one—would occupy the apartment above the church and be treated like a visiting dignitary. For the visiting vicar, the one-month sojourn on Corfu was akin to an exotic paid vacation, the only official business being Sunday sermons. Often the vicar would make this his only business and spend the rest of his time seeing the sights of Corfu and going to the beach. Occasionally a vicar would come who felt it his duty to see to the well-being of the parishioners as well as the needy of the island. It was just such a vicar who had arrived the previous week.

When I approached the circle that had formed around the vicar, he was recounting stories of his visits to the hospital seeing unfortunate foreigners who had met with accident on Corfu. He was saying something about a German man who, when he got the injection in his leg—an injection for what I didn't know—had an allergic reaction and almost lost his leg. When he finished his story I introduced myself and asked what kind of injection the unfortunate German had been given. "The anti-venom serum, of course," the vicar said. "He had been bitten by a snake, a particularly nasty viper. It's the little ones, you know, that are dangerous." Then he told me of an even less fortunate man, a Greek, who had also been bitten by a snake but had arrived at the hospital too late. He had died before the serum had had time to take effect.

"I'm glad it was the Greek who died and not the German," the vicar continued. "I'd much rather send a foreigner home in a hospital plane than in a box. The box is so messy, so much paperwork and the letter to the family and all.

"It doesn't really matter to me what country a foreigner is from or what church he attends. If he's in hospital, I'll try to comfort him. And if he has to go home in the box, I'll see to the details and write the letter to the family. I don't like to—but it's what I must do. The church doesn't send me here just to loll in the sun." He stopped a moment to reflect. Then he said, "And what do you do here on Corfu?"

I was aghast at his matter-of-fact attitude toward 'the box,' especially since I had been so dangerously close to ending up in one myself. I was glad I didn't have to inconvenience him with all those nasty details—the letter home and all. It took me a moment to collect myself. Then I told him of my days in Kontókali and my upcoming move to the monastery.

Next morning, after checking out of the Cyprus Hotel, I went to the house in Kontókali to await Andy and Ann's return. I searched for a good way of breaking bad news to them—the news that their recent arrival would be followed by a hasty departure. But I could think of no good way of being the bearer of such ill tidings. I considered delaying the bad news, letting them live in a state of blissful ignorance a while before telling them of their imminent departure at the insistence of the secret police. But when I saw them coming up the path and ran to greet them, Andy called out to ask if I'd seen any plainclothesmen lurking in the fig trees. He was only joking, of course, but I couldn't help but let the cat out of the bag.

I tried to temper the bad news with the story of the snake and how, even if it were possible for them to remain on Corfu, they would probably want to find another place to live. But that did little to mollify their disappointment; it merely confirmed their growing conviction that Corfu was a crazy place, fit only for madmen. In the end, they felt lucky to be getting out relatively unscathed.

Two days later I helped them take their luggage to town. And as they got into the taxi that would take them to the airport, we bid farewell.

Chapter 11

When I got off the bus at Strinilas the villagers had heard I was coming and knew who I was. They greeted me at the gates of their stone houses. "Up the mountain to the monastery?" they asked me. "You're the friend of the monk?" Children ran after me with fruit.

The great plateau seemed particularly inhospitable under my pack's weight. The sun beat down mercilessly. The final cone of the mountain left me drenched in sweat. When I arrived at the gate, the monk was waiting for me. His face was a single broad smile. His young friend had arrived.

I dropped my pack just outside the door to my cell. The pack fascinated the monk. He tried to lift it with one hand. Its weight impressed him. He inspected the straps and zippers and felt the material. He had never seen anything like it. Then he motioned that he'd like to try it on.

I hoisted the pack to his back and together we got his arms through the straps and hoisted it over his long black robe. As I adjusted the straps, he tested the weight by bobbing his knees. Then he strode off purposefully. He crossed the courtyard with sure and powerful steps, as if he were embarking on a pilgrimage. He strode back, his face radiant.

"Thomás and monk," he said, "we go Mount Athos!" He burst out laughing.

Leaving me to unpack, he went to the kitchen to make coffee. Soon I heard him shout from the kitchen door, "Thomás! Coffee! Come, come!"

I dropped what I was doing and went to the kitchen where the monk had set two cups of coffee on the table and a plate of olives and bread. Over repast, we tried to converse, but it was still quite difficult. My command of his language still rudimentary, our conversation progressed more like an introductory Greek lesson.

"What is this?" I asked, pointing to the cup before me. The monk answered in Greek. Then I formed a short sentence using the new word. "Inside the cup is coffee," I said, to which the monk seemed truly pleased. He patted me on the back. Then we went on to the next word. Progress was slow, but the monk was patient—far more patient than I was. He was a good teacher, and after a few days we were able to talk to each other entire evenings in (fragmented) Greek.

Later that day, searching the courtyard for stones I could use as bookends, I came upon the monk bent over a stone tub. He was washing a robe, and he was up to his elbows in soapy water. Curious what I wanted the stones for, he followed me back to my cell.

He stood in the open doorway and watched me first line the books across the table then prop them up with the stones. I took out my notebooks and pads of paper, pens, pencils, and envelopes, and arranged them neatly. Then I moved the chair to the center of the table and sat.

The monk stepped up to my newly created desk. He looked at my little haven of order and said, "Thomás reads and writes much, no?"

"Yes," I said.

He touched the bindings of some of the books just to feel what English books felt like. Then he picked up the copy of *The Works of Lewis Carrol* and laid it on the desk. Sitting on the bench, he dug deep into his robe and took out his thick, half-frame reading glasses. Lifting his chin so he could peer through them, he rubbed the cloth-bound cover between his fingers and said, "It is good, yes?"

He opened the book and carefully examined the foreign script, his eyes following his fingers across the page. Feeling the page as much as looking at it, he treated it as if it were a rare, old manuscript.

Carefully turning the pages, he came upon the illustration from *Alice in Wonderland* in which a caterpillar sits upon a tremendous toadstool smoking a hookah. I followed his eyes as he studied first the toadstool, then the caterpillar, then the hookah. His gaze went back to the caterpillar and he studied it carefully, his head bent low over the book. He mumbled something beneath his breath.

Then he noticed Alice looking up at the scene from between the blades of grass with a bewilderment matching his own, and he slapped the book shut. He looked up at me and smiled uncertainly. I smiled back, wanting to explain who Alice was and what she was doing there between the blades of grass; but the thought of translating Alice's adventures in Wonderland into Greek boggled my mind. It seemed as fantastic as the adventures themselves.

That evening we had the first of many a dinner that followed a set routine or ritual, the opening gesture of which would come like a large stone being thrown into a small pond as the calm silence of my after-noon was shattered by a loud and shrill, "Thomás! Come! Come here!!" For the first few days I thought something horrible had happened. I came running, ready to tear the sleeve off my shirt to make a tourniquet to stem the bleeding from a nasty wound or to find a board to make a splint to set his broken leg. But always I found him unharmed, busily putting food on the long table, the kitchen full of the rich aromas of garlic, olive oil, and sometimes fish or chicken.

Sometimes his call would find me in my room, where I was absorbed in reading or writing. But more often I heard his cries while sitting on the edge of the monastery wall, gazing at the sun sink silently over the sea to the west, or watching the mountains of Albania fade from pink to dark blue to black. I'd have just achieved an inner silence reflective of this vast scene I was witnessing—no less than the earth rotating upon its axis—when I'd suddenly be called back in as if I were a kite and the monk was hauling in on my line.

"Thomás. Come!" And I would find myself sitting across a long table from this fellow dressed in a long black robe, sparkling eyes shining out of his old and weathered face. We would raise our glasses of the local red wine and say, "To life!"

In the beginning I was under close scrutiny as I ate, my foreign eating habits first noted—and then supplanted—one by one by the Greek habits. At our first dinner we had chicken and potatoes. Since the monk cooked them in a pan half-filled with olive oil, the oil oozed out of the food and slowly filled my plate. When the monk uncorked an old wine bottle and poured more of the thick, golden-brown oil over his plate, I was glad he wasn't looking my way to see my incredulous look, which I was unsuccessfully trying to hide. I was new there and didn't want to offend. When he held the bottle across the table so I, too, could drench my oil-sodden food in yet more oil, I shook my head politely. When he kept his arm stretched across the table, lightly rocking it from side to side, I sighed, dropped my fork, and grabbed the bottle. Letting a few drops fall on my food, I put the bottle down. I picked up my fork and continued eating, not daring to look up to catch the disparaging gaze that he was no doubt casting my way.

I was staring at my plate, stabbing a potato with my fork, when the monk, fully aware I was trying to avert his gaze, called out in his gravely voice, "Thomás." I looked up. He was shaking a finger at me, looking through squinted eyes and laughing.

A few moments passed. Then he picked up a head of garlic, tore off half a dozen cloves, and peeled them with a sharp knife. He popped a few cloves into his mouth, put the rest on the edge of his plate, then held out the head of garlic and the knife to me. I stared at him and said, "No." No monk was going to push me around.

"It is good," he said.

"Yes," I agreed. I indicated how much garlic was already in the food. He backed off.

"Okay," he said cheerfully. "Tomorrow."

"Tomorrow what?" I cried.

"Tomorrow you have more garlic," and he burst out laughing.

Actually, he was right. The next day I did peel a few extra cloves of garlic and ate them with my meal. Within a week, I was drenching my food in olive oil and popping cloves of garlic like candy; and none of it was under duress. A meal just wasn't complete without liberal amounts of both garlic and olive oil.

At the beginning I offered to cook, but it was clear he was afraid of what I might come up with. So he cooked and I did the dishes, which was fine until it grew colder and the wind began to howl. The sink's drainpipe passed directly through the monastery's outer wall and ended in mid-air. The water and debris fell a good twenty feet before hitting the mountain's steep slope. When the wind blew, the pipe caught the wind and a steady stream of cold air blew back in my face along with a good share of the water I had just sent down. When low cloud enshrouded the mountain's peak, the wind would drive the cloud up the drainpipe, turning the sink into a geyser of steam. For some reason the cloud would grow more concentrated inside the room than without, so when I was finished doing the dishes and opened the door to the courtyard, fog would bellow out. Sometimes the wind blew so hard that no water at all would go down, and the center of the sink would be a bubbling, frothing mess. By the time I had finished the dishes and coaxed the water down, my hands would be so numb I'd have to warm them over the gas stove to get the feeling back.

One morning after breakfast the monk informed me that we were to meet Spiros, a mason from Strinilas, to work on a church they were building at the lower monastery. At first I didn't understand what he meant by the lower monastery, so he brought me to the low wall and pointed to the building with the untended terraced fields at the base of the mountain's last cone. He said, "When storm and thunder and lightning comes, we go there." Then he went to the kitchen to gather some food in a sack, which he slung over his shoulder, and together we walked down the hill to the lower monastery.

It is truly curious to observe the process of Greek construction. Though the Greeks are credited as the progenitors of our civilization, somehow, over the centuries, they must have lost the concept of the right angle. I've never yet seen a Greek building outside Athens that can boast a right angle. Objects roll and slide along the floors and the doors hang at an odd pitch. I had often wondered how the Greeks achieved such marvels, but then I met Spiros.

Spiros was an elderly man with an old and worn jacket draped over his shoulders, and a cigarette forever dangling from the corner of his mouth. He was mixing concrete when we arrived, and as he did so he told me that the church, when complete, was to be a one-room stone and cinderblock structure. He had already laid an uneven stone floor, which rose in the back with the slope of the mountain, and built the foundation of the walls, which was composed of bits of broken rock mortared together into a uniform and level surface. Accuracy at the foundation level was important, because any mistakes here would cause the cinderblock walls to curve inwardly or outwardly and leave spaces in the walls where no spaces should be. The holes would then have to be filled with bits of stone cut to size. Our job was to find these stones for Spiros.

I loved watching Spiros work, and it was obvious that the monk had recruited him for his expertise in stone work. Though the walls he had built were not straight, he could cut a stone to fit any size hole. He was a master at patchwork. He had a knack for finding the fault lines in a stone and he knew exactly the right angle and force with which to let his hammer fall. It was with great joy that he seized a stone, examined it from all angles, and tapped it with his hammer. He extracted the greatest satisfaction when a stone complied to the minimum of force.

When they were reasonably sure I could fetch stones as Spiros need-ed them, the monk went inside to prepare lunch. Occasionally Spiros would yell out "*Megalo*" or "*Micros,*" large or small, and he would point to where he wanted a pile. Then I would go off and collect more stones.

Once I had piled enough stones to keep Spiros going for a while, I went inside to explore the lower monastery, where in stormy weather the monk and I would seek shelter. It was an old farmhouse, the place where the people had lived who cultivated the surrounding terraced fields and no doubt tended flocks of sheep and goats that grazed the mountain's slopes. The walls of the house were three feet thick, and the windows had wide sills. The doorways were low, so low I had to stoop to pass through them, as if the house had been built for a shorter race of people. A warmth filled the house that the monastery lacked. Perhaps this was because a family had lived here or because the rooms were connected and you needn't pass outside to go from room to room. I immediately felt safe and secure in this house and felt it a wise decision on the monk's part that we would come here when storms raged on the mountain.

The layout of the house was quite simple. When you walked in the front door you were in a hallway. To the left was what was once the dining room, in the center of which was a large wooden table surrounded by chairs. In each corner of the room was a door that opened to a bedroom. Off the monk's bedroom, which was in the far left-hand corner, was a smaller room, a shrine, to which the monk would retire for an hour or so in the afternoons to say his prayers.

If you went right upon entering the house you came to the kitchen. Like the kitchen in the upper monastery, it was exceedingly simple. There was a shelf on which were dishes and cooking utensils. There was a two-burner gas stove and a stone sink. Above the sink was a tin vessel that we filled with water from the well. It had a valve at the bottom to let water out as needed. Above the sink was a window. The only table was about knee high and rickety. There were a few small chairs, stools, and benches.

The nicest feature of the kitchen, which made it far more comfortable than the one in the upper monastery, was a small fireplace. Sometimes it smoked horribly, especially when the wind blew hard, but it let out a warm golden-yellow glow that warmed me to the marrow on the stormiest of days. An iron tripod held a big pot over the fire in which many a fine meal slowly cooked. These were meals that had the delicate seasoning of wood smoke added to the usual flavors of garlic, oregano, and olive oil.

Soon I heard the monk's familiar call, "Thomás, Spiros. *Ora Fayitú!*" Mealtime. Spiros came inside, and the monk laid out a delicious meal of chicken, rice, and greens. The monk poured wine. I tried to follow their conversation but didn't have much luck, though I suspected they were talking about me most of the time.

After lunch I began to gather the dirty dishes, but the monk told me to stop. He had me follow him to the front hallway, where he found a pencil stub and a scrap of paper on a windowsill and wrote a note in Greek. He handed it to me and told me to go to the village and give it to the man in the *kafeneon*.

Armed with the monk's note, a good meal under my belt, and wine coursing through my veins, I set out for the village, the sound of Spiros smashing stones to fit holes fading behind me.

The old men of the village were assembled at the village *kafeneon*. They had pulled chairs out onto the street where the sun's rays could warm them. They were a motley crew, half of them leaning on canes and all of them talking at the top of their lungs and gesticulating wildly. Finding the proprietor, I handed him the note, which he read carefully. Then he yelled something up an alleyway behind the shop. His wife came, took the note, and went back up the alleyway. Then he showed me a seat in the center of the group of old men.

A ripple of "*Filos tu papa*," friend of the priest, spread through the crowd. An old geezer to my right, who had a cigarette dangling out of the corner of his mouth and a cup of coffee balanced upon his knee, stared me in the eye then launched into a raving monologue, not a word of which I understood. Gesticulating wildly, he pointed up the mountain then at the sun then at the big tree in the square, then down at me. He made as if he had a long beard and he stroked it thoughtfully. He closed his eyes as if he were absorbed in deep contemplation. All the while words were cascading from his mouth like water from a waterfall. I became dizzy. The other old men were so concentrated upon this man and his story that they all but forgot me; that is, until the man suddenly fell silent and they all turned to me as if they expected me to respond with an equal flash of wit.

It was all I could do to stammer out the words, "I speak little Greek."

With this there was a single burst of uncontrolled hysterics from all quarters as the man who had just finished his monologue dropped his cigarette—which had been dangling so precariously from the corner of his mouth—onto his pants. When he swiped it of, his cup of coffee along with its delicate little saucer, which had been so skillfully balanced on his knee, went crashing to the ground.

All hell started to break loose and I was eyeing routes of escape when the proprietor called me into the *kafeneon*, saving me from who knows what. He sat me at a table and poured us each a large glass of brandy.

When we had drained the contents of our glasses he placed in my hands a big bag of locally gathered wild greens he called *horta*, a loaf of bread wrapped in a fine linen napkin, and a bag of eggs. He indicated I was to take them up the mountain. I said farewell to the men outside. They laughed again at the sight of me. And with their laughter fading behind me, I left the village and made my way back up the mountain.

That evening after dinner, the monk pulled a deck of cards out of his robe's deep pocket and taught me the game the men always played at the Chess Café. He shuffled the cards, placed four cards face up on the table, then cut the deck. He gave me but a fleeting glance of the card chosen then dealt out the remainder of the deck.

He went first. The first card in his stack was a seven. He matched his seven with a seven overturned on the table then took both cards and started a new pile by his side. Then I turned over my top card. It was a four and matched no card on the table. I showed it to him, he took up an ace and a three from the table, showed me that they added up to four, and thus I started my own pile of tricks. His turn; he had a six. Since only a jack remained, he left his six overturned next to the jack. Then it was my turn again. We played until he ran out of cards to turn over; it was time to count points. Since my stack was bigger than his, I assumed I had won. I counted my cards and had thirty-five. He counted his, did some calculations in his head, then wrote down an eight on a little scrap of paper. Then he took up my cards, counted them, did his mental calculations, and wrote down a four next to his eight. I didn't understand why he had gotten eight points while I got only four, but I let it pass; I would get the hang of it soon enough. But as we played more hands and he consistently came up with twice as many points than me, I began to object.

I asked him, "*Yiatí?*" why?

He acted as if he didn't understand what my problem was.

"*Yiatí?*" I asked again.

"*Yiatí? Yiatí.*" He responded. *Yiatí* means both why and because.

As we played into the night he became increasingly smug. Finally, when I threatened to quit, he broke down and showed me how he scored. So many points for the most cards, so many for the jack of hearts, so many for the card picked when cutting the deck, and so many for going out first.

Finally armed with the rules, I won the next game. He acted as if it were just luck. But then I won the next game and the one after that. Finally he quit. I had beat him at his own game. We never played cards again.

ॐ   ॐ

I quickly found that no day on the mountain ended as I pictured it at its inception. Often the radical digressions my day would take were caused by a certain dimension of mystery rooted in the barrier of language. The most common harbinger of digression was the monk's commanding call, "*Éla mázi mu,*" come with me. Whenever he said this, I became immediately attentive to his every move and gesture so I might have the best chance of solving the conundrum his subsequent actions would place before me.

Though there were many examples of this, one in particular stands out in my mind. It was a quiet day in the upper monastery and I had spent the morning writing. Around noon, after eating lunch with the monk, I was sitting at my desk with a cup of coffee, ready to resume my work, when the monk came in, said "*Éla mázi mu,*" and walked out. I sprang to my feet and reached the door just in time to see the tail end of his robe going through the kitchen door. I got to the kitchen to find him half inside one of the cabinets, looking as if he were trying to hide in there. But he was rummaging. He finally came out holding a couple of natural sponges and an array of rags.

He grunted, signaling that I should take them; then he removed a bucket from the cabinet and I thought to myself, 'Ah-ha, we're going to wash something,' and when he finally stood and handed me a mop, a broom, and a dustpan my guess seemed confirmed.

Armed with these cleaning implements, I followed him across the courtyard to the church and into a closet behind the altar where he started rummaging through all sorts of junk—old candleholders, broken pieces of statues, dust-covered wooden crates—until he came up with a long length of rope.

Back outside he had me hold one end of the rope as he held the other end. He walked several paces then, without warning, tugged on his end, tearing the rope from my hands. "Thomás," he grunted. He motioned that I should hold on tightly. We pulled against each other until he was certain of the rope's strength. Coiling the rope, he slung it over his shoulder and walked back into the kitchen. I wondered where the rope fit in and became all the more baffled when he took off his robe and rolled up his pant legs and shirtsleeves. He took off his shoes and socks, left his hat on the table, slung the rope over his shoulder again, and stepped back outside. I followed him across the courtyard and behind the church. Tying one end of the rope around his waist with a secure knot, he handed the other end to me. Then he jumped up on the low rim of a stone well and pointed down into the deep, stone-lined darkness. I quickly took up the slack, and before I knew it I was bracing my feet on the well's rim, lowering the monk into the darkness, bits of broken rock and gravel splashing beneath him. I had played out a good dozen feet of rope when I heard his feet splashing into water. Then the rope slackened.

Peering into the darkness, I saw the monk knee deep in stagnant water. He untied the rope from around his waist and yelled up to me. It was a word I was unfamiliar with. He repeated the word, but, alas, an unknown word does not become intelligible through repetition. I told him to wait and ran to my room for my pocket dictionary. As I ran back across the courtyard I heard him screaming frantically, "Thomás! Thomás! *Éla!*" Come! The poor man thought he'd been abandoned. And even in that darkness I could see the look of relief when I peered over the edge of the well once again. I said, "What is it you want?" He repeated the word, which translated as *bucket*. I should have known. He thought so, too.

I tied the bucket onto the end of the rope and lowered it into the well. He filled it with water and sludge. I hoisted it, dumped it out, and lowered it again. We extracted dozens of buckets of water in this manner until not enough water remained to fill the bucket. I then lowered the sponges, rags, mop, and broom to him. Then I sat down to rest. I waited for him to call me to lift the bucket out. The sludge became increasingly slimy and thick.

Once, when he called me, I glared down at him in the darkness. "What do you want?" I asked. "Food? Wine? A blanket? Oh, you sleep down there tonight?" He got mad and yelled, "The water, the water, out. Now!" and I pulled up another bucket of slime.

I was resting with my back against the rim of the well, waiting for him to call my name, when he yelled out, "*Lepta!*" Money! I looked down the well. He was digging, and between his fingers were little flashes of silvery light. He started dancing down there at the bottom of the muddy well like a man who struck gold. He dug like a madman, deeper and deeper, coming up with more and more coins. He rinsed the coins in the last little puddle of water before putting them into the bucket. By the time he had cleaned the well to its smooth rock bottom, I had hauled out two buckets full of coins—worth almost one hundred dollars.

The next day the coins were outside drying in the sun when some Greeks from the mainland came to visit the monastery. They thought we were making a collection and dropped spare change onto the pile.

Chapter 12

It was well before sunrise, and I was sitting on the wall that over-looked the mist-enshrouded mountains of Albania. At this early hour, with the sun but a dim intimation, Albania was suffused in fading starlight.

The sun rose fiery behind the mountains, its rays striking first the Albanian peaks and then the tip of Pantokrator. The valleys still slumbered in darkness. The stretch of sea between Corfu and the mainland was still cloaked in night. The mist cleared from the Albanian peaks and slowly, as the sun mounted the sky, the sharp valleys of Albania grew distinct.

Since coming to the mountain I had developed a heightened power of concentration. I had grown patient, as patient as the monk. But it wasn't the monk who taught me this patience. His was but an example. We drew patience from the same source: the mountain itself.

It was in times like these, times of uninterrupted gazing at the vast expanses, that the wheels slowed enough for the mountain to speak. The mountain was immobile, existing without a thought. The mountain was silent, and within that silence was an invitation. On the mountain I had no choice but to refrain from unnecessary talk. This outward stillness was an invitation for me to take that step—imperceptible to outward gaze—into inner silence. In silence, one casts off all that is unnecessary; in silence all that is frivolous, inessential, and superfluous naturally falls away. What one is left with is the essential.

During lunch the monk told me he would spend the night in the village. The next day was Sunday, and every Sunday, early in the morning, he performed Mass at the village church. Shortly after we finished eating,

I watched him, a black figure with a little bag over his shoulder, fading to a dot as he went down the steep switchbacks, by the lower monastery, and across the gray plateau.

Every step he took increased by exactly one pace the distance between another human being and myself, and with every step I felt that much more my elemental connection to the mountain. By the time he had disappeared over the edge of the plateau, that connection was complete. I was now alone with the mountain.

Late that afternoon I was writing at my desk when I looked up from the page to see the room being plunged into darkness. I glanced out the window, but the window had fogged, or so I thought, for all was a uniform shade of dark gray. I could see neither the stunted trees in the courtyard nor the building on the other side. I opened the door, but that did nothing to better the visibility. A cool blast of heavy, foggy air rushed into the room, saturating the room with moisture; I felt my beard and it was wet.

Crossing the threshold, I entered the dense, windblown cloud, which penetrated my skin and burrowed deep into my bones. Walking to the low wall beyond the kitchen, I was met straight on with a full-force gale, a gale of pea-soup fog, of low cloud pierced by high mountain.

The fog defined a circle through which my eyes could not penetrate. Beneath me the wall faded before reaching the rocky slope, and even my hands looked less sharp than they had inside. Before, all had been keenly defined: my hand holding the pen, the pen's sharp point touching the paper, the letters forming into words on the page. It had all been so clear, so black and white. I knew how one word would be followed by the next and how upon the foundation of the last the next would build. But that continuity had been broken. The light had dimmed. I had stepped outside into opacity, a world at once less defined and more immediate.

Here was no intermediary, no screen through which the mind could pigeonhole reality. Here, at the edge of a sea of nothingness, clutching a wall that faded into insubstantiality, my feet anchored in a ground that seemed no longer foundational, the mind was bypassed by the marrow.

It was as if I were the lookout on a ship's prow, peering into the shadowless obscurity, looking for a nuance of something tangible by which to guide my ship. The mist, like a continual spray, drove the water deep into my clothes and made me shiver. I awaited the massive wave that would crash over me. I awaited the shudder that would resonate through the ship's hull. But no wave came. The rock beneath my feet remained firm, though it faded so quickly from sight.

Then came an opening, a crack in the fog. I was staring straight up the edge of a vertical column of cloud, a puffy cottony wall, towering, threatening to tumble hundreds of feet onto my head. The top glowed pink, red, and golden from the sun, which was setting, no doubt peacefully, beyond the tumult. It was a sudden reminder of the continuity of astronomical cycles unaffected by the happenings down below. Then the column closed, and the circle closed in on me again.

I went inside to find my jacket. I put on my hat and gloves. The simple passing of clouds, which from a village along the coast was a fleeting phenomenon of the sky, was from the monastery a spectacular event full of immediacy. This was the layer of the atmosphere in which warm and cold met and played out their battle. From where I was there was no observation, it was all participation.

When I went back out to the wall it was as if my ship had been dashed upon the shore: I was on an island surrounded by a sea of white, a white of turbulence and change. The cone of Pantokrator was bathed in the last reddened rays of the setting sun, clean and shining as if it had been washed by the cloud. But my island illusion didn't last, for suddenly the sea lifted in great puffy veils of movement and engulfed me, leaving me submerged once again.

Then, as if the great sea that I was in the bottom of was parting, hues of blue peeked out high overhead and the sky was revealed again, only to be obliterated a moment later by a wave of crashing cloud. From being a creature of the land, upon an island in an expanse of white, I became a creature of the seas, practically drinking the air through my mouth-gills. Then, as the clouds parted, I became a creature of the sky, an eagle soaring high over the island of Corfu.

Each time the sea of white opened around me I could see a line of clouds growing in the distance, boiling internally and mounting to terrific heights. And as the last light of the sun faded, these nearing clouds shone with flashes of their own light. They were thunderheads coming my way, and before them the wind howled. The air became charged. And just before the wall of seething cloud slammed into the mountain, the wind, which had been rushing out ahead of the storm, suddenly switched direction and started rushing toward the cloud. The oncoming thunderhead was consuming the surrounding air, sucking the air into it, sucking the mountain into its sphere as well. Suddenly I was in the middle of the seething cross-currents of the cloud's interior, my skin bitten by rain driven horizontally now over the monastery wall.

The ferocity of the storm drove me from that wall into the courtyard's interior. Wind and rain buffeted me from all sides. It was all I could do to keep my balance in the whirlwind. I huddled against a wall just to feel something solid, something rooted in the earth, something unchanging.

Gusts eddied around unseen corners, hitting me like the disembodied souls of the monastery's former inhabitants. They came out of the gray like cool hands upon the back of my neck, making my spine tingle with waves of sensation. With my mind unhinged by the tempest, I did not know whether it was from the cold and the wet or from these hands whipping out of the whirlwind that these waves of sensation flowed over me. I turned with a start, certain that someone had tapped me on the shoulder. But the same gray was staring back at me.

The rushing wind made the monastery's mute stone speak. The top of the monastery wall moaned with a hollow sound, and the buildings howled furiously, as if scores of multi-pitched and out of tune strings were being played with varying intensity by a thousand bows. No one string could be discerned out of the mismatched chorus. The droning in my ears never reached a crescendo, never found resolution as the ever-rising wind drove the cold and rain ever deeper into my bones.

The whole while that I was being tossed by the storm, enclosed in a tiny ball of gray, stumbling like a nearsighted fool, walking into walls

and being buffeted by the eddies of wind forming off the corners of
the buildings, I was aware too that I was over half a mile above the sea,
over an hour and a half from the nearest human being, running around
beneath thick walls, on a mountain in the center of a thunderhead. The
whole while I was in the thick of it, I was also strangely outside of it,
aware—graphically, spatially, with the clarity of looking down on a topo-
graphical map—of exactly where I was. While never losing for an instant
the sharp immediacy of my surroundings, I could practically see the great
globe itself and where I stood on it.

My greatest security came from knowing I was within the confines of
high stone walls that had weathered the storms of over half a millennium.
But this security faded when the distant rumbles I had taken little account
of grew louder than the howling wind. Fear overtook me as the thick fog
became illuminated with blinding flashes of light that lacked direction of
origin, flashes that illuminated equally my entire field of perception with
a ghostly light. Flash followed flash, followed by echoing rumbles.

I decided to take my bearings and head inside.

But it was too late.

A crash of unimaginable magnitude shook the mountain to its very
foundations, a crash that was concurrent with a blinding flash that rendered my eyes useless for a few agonizing moments, moments during
which another clap of thunder crashed around me followed by another
and yet another. The lightning bolts were distinct now through the thick
fog, arcing less than a hundred feet above my head. They were close
enough to gauge their thickness—thick as a man's arm, thick as a horse's
torso. Others originated *below* me and shot up the side of the mountain,
branching directly overhead. Their zigzag paths were etched on my reti-
nas, etched in burning red.

Panic seized me to the marrow, wiping out all sense of sport I had felt
toward the storm. It was no longer a playful game to be walking in the
tempest. So I ran, trying to anticipate the next bolt of lightning. I knew if
I stopped I would be hit. I ran like a jackrabbit dodging the hunter's shot,
all the while hearing the boom, boom, boom from all directions. I came

to a high wall and ran alongside it until it turned a corner away from me. I missed it, ran straight on, and was again at sea without an anchor or point of reference.

The storm rendered my will inoperative; in its place was pure and raw instinct, an instinct as old as time itself, the instinct that calls out from the primal depths for shelter. I became a being in search of a cave, a niche, or a burrow in which to find protection from the storm.

And then, off in the distance, I heard, between claps of thunder, the eerie sound of something ringing. I ran toward the sound and it became more distinct. I recognized it: it was the bell that hung over the monastery's front gate. What manner of being could be out on a night like this? It must be the monk. He has returned, found me missing, and now he's calling me back! Or perhaps it was more of those cool hands that had brushed me on the back of the neck.

I followed the sound to the gate. I stared into the flashing darkness, searching desperately for an outlined figure. But no figure was there beneath the bell, just the rope flying in the frenzy of the wind. The storm itself was ringing the bell. Knowing now where I was, I quickly found my room and slid in through the door.

Chapter 13

In the morning all the elements of the storm were still there: the terrific wind, the driving rain, the impenetrable fog. Thunder could be heard in the distance, echoing off the mountains of Albania. I wondered what the weather was like below, in Corfu Town or in Kontókali. I imagined that it was raining. Nothing more. I recalled the many rainy days I had spent in Kontókali, looking longingly at the mountain, its summit lost in thick cloud. It had always looked peaceful like that, piercing through our turbulent and stormy weather, so still and unmoving in the distance.

I mused over the scene that was no doubt playing out at the Chess Café—the old men arriving one by one, shaking their umbrellas outside the door and sitting down for a serious game of cards; the proprietor's son dodging rain puddles to bring ouzo to shop owners down the street. I could imagine all of this but it seemed absurd to do so. Every hour I spent on the mountain increased by a thousand miles the distance between the rest of Corfu and myself. I felt as close to the old Greek men in the Chess Café as I did to the people I had seen meandering through the streets of Spanish towns, or to the people in the bazaars of India, whom I had never seen, or to my parents sitting in their kitchen sipping coffee and listening to the classical radio show. The rest of the world, everything that existed outside the confines of the monastery walls, seemed a rather flimsy abstraction. I began to wonder where I would end up if I climbed out of the monastery, down the rocky slope, pierced back through the bottom of the clouds, and reentered the land of men. And what language would they be speaking there? Swahili? Hindi? Chinese? Any of these seemed as likely to me as Greek.

As to the question of what language they spoke in the world beneath the cloud, the answer came, not by my going down, but by an emissary coming up.

I was in the kitchen, sipping a cup of coffee.

"Thomás. Thomás!"

My name rang out above the cry of the wind. I opened the kitchen door and admitted not only a cool and wet blast of fog, but also the monk, looking rather forlorn and speaking Greek at an alarmingly fast rate. The only words I could understand were the words for cold, lightning, thunder, rain, and wind. In all, he summed up my sentiments exactly; what else was there to say?

I offered to make him coffee.

"No!" he boomed. "We go below. Down. Down. Lower monastery. Now! Thunder coming, lightning coming. Lightning bad, very bad. We go NOW!"

He whirled around the kitchen like a dervish, shoveling bread, coffee, rice, chickpeas, sugar, olives, garlic, and any other food he could find into a cloth sack. Then he buttoned his shawl-like coat and we burst out into the storm, each going to our own cells. I emptied my bag onto my bed and refilled it with what I'd need at the lower monastery. The monk burst into my room, the food sack in one hand and a sack of clothes in the other. Rain dripped from his robe, forming a puddle on the floor. His eyes flashed menacingly. "Now!" he yelled. "We go now!"

We burst back out into the storm, closed the monastery gate behind us, and started down Pantokrator's steep slope. Bending our bodies sharply into the cutting wind and rain, we kept our heads bowed as if in veneration to the storm.

When we burst through the door at the lower monastery and closed it behind us, a cold wind followed us in through a crack beneath the door. It emitted a high-pitched and eerie whine, a whistle that rose and fell with every gust. The stone house was stone-cold, but it was solid; it was a safe refuge. Never has a sailor in a wild sea felt more relieved to set foot on solid land.

First we cleaned the room that would be mine. There was a single bed, a desk, a chair, and a large window. It was so dark outside that the monk had to hold a lantern while I swept the room. When the monk shook out the blankets on the bed, a dead scorpion fell to the floor. He kicked it under the bed, thinking I hadn't seen it. After that, I was always careful not to let my blankets dangle on the floor.

I followed the monk through the hallway toward the kitchen, the circle of light emitted by the lantern casting a grotesquely enlarged shadow of the monk's billowing robe on the walls and ceiling. It preceded us like a dark phantom.

In the kitchen, the monk closed the door to the hallway and let out a thankful sigh. He lit another lantern and placed it on the windowsill above the sink; the added glow of the lantern made the room actually seem warm. The monk built a fire in the fireplace. We pulled the bench up to the fire and stretched out our hands to within inches of the flame. We stared into the crackling fire and let its warmth penetrate every pore of our bodies. Steam rose from our rain-drenched clothes.

Outside, the storm was heightening. The monk donned his heavy black cloak, and I followed him to the front door where an old and patched cloak hung from a hook. He put the cloak around my shoulders and bid me to tie it tightly. He thrust a bucket into my hand and pushed open the door. He brought me to the well, and as I lowered the bucket he gathered an armful of wood piled under the roof's small overhang. Hauling the bucket from the well, I nervously eyed the overflowing metal tank for collecting rainwater that stood upon a scaffold towering above the outhouse. It was a perfect lightning conductor. I ran, the monk close behind me, back into the lower monastery.

We sat again before the fire, feet and hands outstretched, our benumbed extremities slowly gaining feeling. We watched again the steam rise from our clothes as the storm overtook the mountain and pounded its slopes with rain, hail, and thick bolts of lightning. Violent claps of thunder shook the mountain as the howling wind traveled down the chimney in bursts, as if driven by a piston. The room filled with smoke. The monk put a handful of loose black tea into a battered teakettle. He added sugar and filled the pot with water. Then he put the pot directly into the hot, glowing coals.

A little later, still sitting on the low bench before the fire, teacups balanced on our knees, the monk said, "Thomás, the fire is good. Yes?"

"Yes, it is good. It is warm. Outside is cold. There is rain, wind, thunder—and lightning. Outside is bad; here is good."

"Yes, Thomás. Outside is bad, but here it is good."

We were staring at the embers, occasionally adding a stick to the fire. The monk placed an iron tripod into the fireplace and freshened the fire under it. He filled an iron pot with water and put it on the tripod. We poured a bag of chickpeas onto the table and sorted out the sticks and small stones. He poured the chickpeas into the water as I sliced onions. Then he peeled garlic. When we added these ingredients to the boiling water, along with half a bottle of olive oil, the brew was complete but for a few hours of boiling.

"Thomás," the monk said, "when the storm is over you come with me to the church in the village. I baptize you. You become Greek Orthodox, and one day you become *papa*. Yes, *Papa* Thomás. And you can live here, and when I am old you can take care of me. And when I die, this will be your monastery. It is good here, yes?"

"Yes, it is," I replied. "But Thomás no *papa*. One day I go home. I see my family. I see my friends."

"Eh, Thomás," he said and shook his finger at me. "I baptize you and all is good. You won't *have* to go home. You stay here and I teach you about Christ. We eat rice and fish and we build rooms, and on Sundays you come with me to village and I teach you. The people in the village like you. They think you be good *papa*. One day you have long hair and long beard and black robe like me. We walk together to the village. Everybody who sees us bows their head and says, 'There are the two *papáthes*, one old and one young. Long live Christ!' They give us food. When we bless the olive press they give us oil, and the best oil, too.

"Come, I show you."

He got up with a grunt, thrust the lantern into my hand, and I followed him out of the kitchen into the front hallway. He opened an old wooden door, which had rotted off its hinges. He had to lift it and lean it against the wall so we could enter. He lit a match and put it to the wick of a kerosene lantern, which sputtered and sizzled before taking the flame. The room was long and narrow and cold like a cave, yet it was dry. Along the walls were shelves from floor to ceiling packed with dusty tins, bottles, kegs, and urns.

"Look," he said, pointing at the dust-covered tins. He tapped one after another with his knuckle to show that they were all full. "Olive oil, olive oil, olive oil—much oil. Too much oil. More oil than *I* can use." He found an old and rusted nail on the ground, pried the lid off a tin, and stuck his finger in. It emerged dripping with golden-green oil. He stuck his finger into his mouth.

"Mmm," he said, "very good!" He motioned for me to do the same. The oil tasted delicious.

Then he moved deeper into the room and pointed at the big earthenware urns. "Olives, olives, olives," he said, shaking his clenched fist, his voice rising. "All full!" He uncorked an urn and scooped out a handful of dripping olives. "You like, yes?"

They *were* delicious, but I was afraid he would link an affirmative answer to my wanting to become a *papa* so I might receive these gifts from the villagers on a regular basis. He looked at me expectantly, waiting for my judgment on the olives and, by association, my decision to become a *papa* and live out his last years with him.

Of course I was flattered. Yet I knew I couldn't accept his offer.

"Yes," I said, "the olives are good, but '*Papa* Thomás' no. I don't want to be a *papa*."

He banged the big cork back into the urn with his fist and blew the lamp out.

"Thélis na fáme?" "Do you want to eat?" the monk asked. The bubbling pot had caused the window above the sink to fog. Drops were forming and gently rolling down the panes.

The monk scooped chickpeas with a wooden ladle into two ceramic bowls as I sliced a few pieces of bread, put a head of garlic on the cutting board, and our meal was ready. He crossed himself and we began to eat. We looked at each other across the table as a downdraft sent smoke into the room. The fire crackled. Sparks flew.

"In Greek, what do you call these," I asked, pointing to the chickpeas in my spoon.

"*Revéthia*," he answered. Then he asked timidly, "And in English?"

"Chickpeas," I answered.

"Cheeek-pays," he said, trying to get his Greek tongue around the word.

"No, not cheeek-pays, chickpeas."

He tried again and said the word perfectly.

"Very good!" I exclaimed.

A broad smile crossed his face and he repeated the word over and over in a sing-song voice, "Chick-peas, chick-peas, chickpeas!" He triumphed in learning a new English word.

He often asked me the English word for something after I asked him the Greek, but usually he forgot it as quickly as he learned it. Not this time. After we had finished our peas and were sopping up the last juices from the bottom of our bowls with thick slices of bread, he suddenly yelled out, "Chickpeas!" and burst out laughing. His laughter was like a lion's roar; it came from deep down inside his belly, from somewhere in the center of his existence.

That evening, as the storm raged outside, we spent hours talking and roasting chestnuts over the coals. The chestnuts burned our fingers as we pried them from their shells.

Chapter 14

The next morning my peaceful dream was cut short by a ghastly clap of thunder whose vanishing echoes took with them the fading images that still graced my closed eyes. As the receding rumble of thunder gave way to the sound of rain driving against the bedroom window, a relentless wind threw its strength against the stone house. Outside, storm clouds as thick as cotton rushed past my window. I couldn't help wondering whether the entire world was pummeled by the storm, or whether the storm sat over this mountain alone. It took an act of will to get out of bed and slip on my clothes.

When I opened the door to the kitchen I was met with a warm and welcoming air. The fire was crackling, and the monk sat in front of it boiling coffee.

Thunder crashed, no doubt originating from a bolt of lightning that struck close by on the mountain's flanks. The monk moaned and shook his head.

"Bad," he said wearily. "Lightning is bad."

His hands trembled as he poured coffee into two cups. This worried me. I had imagined that the monk, having lived on the mountain so many years, was used to raging storms. I had always thought the gods—or God—was watching over him and that that protection was extended to me by my proximity. But to see him so visibly shaken shook my own confidence, especially when I realized I had to take a trip to the outhouse.

It was amid a terrific crash of thunder that I announced I had to go outside. The monk, looking up from his cup of coffee, offered me some advice—mainly about making great haste—and he offered me his winter cloak as protection from the storm. He walked me to the front hallway, and as he unlatched the front door a terrific blast of wind tore the door from his hands. Swinging back on its hinges, it hit the wall with a clamor. I stood a moment, poised, ready to run, waiting for a flash of lightning and a crash of thunder. I wanted to go just after one release of electricity and—hopefully—return before the next.

The lightning came with a nearly simultaneous crack of thunder. The monk bid me good luck.

Actually he said, "May God be with you!"

I ran as fast as I could to the outhouse.

I did my business quickly, thinking all the while of the metal water tank a few feet from where I now squatted.

I was running back to the house when a presentiment of electricity came over me. I stopped and turned to see a bolt of lightning as thick as a horse's hind leg kick out of the sky and strike the tank then branch out and splinter over the outhouse. Thunder crashed simultaneously, as if the heavens themselves were cracking open. The next thing I knew I was inside and safe from the storm. I stood trembling before the monk.

"The storm is bad, no?" he said.

"Yes, it is bad."

Two days later when I awoke the storm had let up. The clouds had lifted and we could see the upper monastery on the mountain's peak. The thunder and lightning had departed, to wreak havoc on other mountains. Only a light drizzle remained.

After breakfast I followed the monk outside to the stone church we had been building with Spiros. The building's floor was made of the mountain's living rock and sloped with the mountain's contour. Our job was to level the floor by pounding the stone with heavy sledgehammers. It was difficult work; the rock barely yielded to our blows. Occasionally our sledgehammers produced a tiny stone chip, but mostly what we produced was a fine stone dust. I pounded away at one spot for over an hour and hardly saw any progress. It was a job difficult to imagine being undertaken anywhere else but on that mountain, where time's daily round was backed up by eternity.

The plaintive braying of a donkey announced the arrival of a man from the village. He jumped from the beast's back and ran to the monk, his face contorted with grief. He spoke quickly to the monk and soon the grief and shock on the villager's face was mirrored on my friend's.

"Thomás," the monk said, "the storm has taken a life. A man from the village was bringing his sheep to shelter when lightning came out of a cloud and made him fall. It happened two days ago. They couldn't reach me because of the storm. Now I must go to the church to pray for him. I will not be back for a few days. Go to the upper monastery. I will meet you there."

The monk rushed inside and reappeared a few moments later with a sack of clothes. He sat sidesaddle on the donkey, and the man from the village led the donkey back down the mountain.

My room at the upper monastery was just as I remembered it: cool and damp. My belongings were in the disarray of my quick departure. After putting things back in order I lay on my bed and fell soundly asleep.

By late afternoon the sky had cleared and the sunset was spectacular. I leaned over the wall and watched the sun sink into the sea. To the east the mountains of Albania glowed pink and red, and as the sun touched the horizon the shadow of Pantokrator crossed the narrow channel and clothed the Albanian mountains in darkness. Twilight deepened. Lights came on in the villages along the coast, mirroring the stars in the sky.

Two days later in the afternoon I was bent over my desk with a pencil in my hand when I heard footsteps in the courtyard. I ran to the door to see the monk crossing the courtyard with a thick stack of wooden planks balanced upon his shoulder. Over his other shoulder was his cloth sack, and looped through his arms were plastic bags filled with vegetables. In his free hand he held a large jug of wine. I ran to him and together we lowered the planks to the ground. Then we sat on the step at the front of the church.

"The man who died," the monk said, "was a good man. He was young, too. He left a wife and two children. It will be difficult for his family, but the people of the village are good people. They will take care of them. I spent two days in the church praying. I have not slept. I am very tired."

"What is the wood for?" I asked him, wondering how he had made it up the mountain under such a load.

"Building," he answered.

"Where did you get it?"

His eyes sparkled. He tapped a crooked finger to his temple. With a mischievous look he said, "To be a monk, Thomás, you must be *Ponirós! Ponirós* Thomás, *PONIRÓS!!*" and he roared with laughter.

I had my pocket dictionary with me. *Ponirós* means "sly."

"Eh," I said, "you *are ponirós*. You are the *Ponirós* Monk!" and I shook my finger at him, as he had shaken his finger at me so many times before.

Then he asked me what the word was in English. I told him.

"Sly," he repeated after me, getting it right the first time. "Sly, sly, sly, slyeee," he said, squinting his eyes at me. "Thomás, I am not sly, you are sly. You are a sly young man. You are a sly chickpea!" He almost rolled off the step, he was laughing so hard. "A sly chickpea!"

It was good to have him back.

Chapter 15

A few weeks passed, a time of quiet and study, of wonderful meals with abundant amounts of olive oil and garlic eaten with the monk.

Then our larder grew thin, so I suggested I go down to Corfu Town to replenish our supplies. The monk agreed. Instead of going to the village to take a bus to town, I decided to walk straight down the eastern slope of the mountain to the coast road, where I could easily catch a ride to town. I chose this route—more difficult by far—both in order to slowly ease myself back into civilization and because there was an abandoned village in this direction at the base of the mountain's cone I wanted to explore. My plan was to spend the night in Corfu Town, shop in the morning, then take the bus back to Strinilas in the afternoon.

The way to the abandoned village was rough. I had to negotiate huge boulders and loose scree. Constantly putting a foot on ground that gave way, I caused many a small avalanche. About halfway to the village I came upon a tiny cave, at the mouth of which was a circle of charred rocks and burnt twigs, a place where goatherds found shelter when overtaken by a storm or when the weather turned cold.

Then I spied a goatherd below me. I hoped our paths would cross. Perhaps he was the goatherd I had shared my meal with the first time I climbed the mountain. Though goatherds often grazed their animals on the mountain's slopes, I had never met another. They were as elusive as the wind. Sometimes in the middle of the night I'd be awakened by goats' bells in the monastery's courtyard. In the morning I would wonder whether I had dreamt it until I saw the goat droppings on the stone flagging.

The goatherd was sitting on a rock watching over his flock. I angled toward him. But when he saw me coming he got up and led his goats away. I wanted to call out to him, but always he remained just out of earshot. Like a wild animal, he shied away.

The abandoned village was nestled in a little valley, a pause on the mountain's steep descent to the sea. It was surrounded by terraced fields now overgrown with bushes, vines, and trees. The silence of the graveyard hung low over the village, and the air was suffused with a forsaken desolation.

Roofs were caved in and stitched over with vines. The church stood on top of a little knoll near the village center, its simple white adobe belfry covered with vines that were slowly tightening their grip and making it crumble.

Jumping over a low wall, I found myself in the courtyard of a large stone house, in the middle of which stood a fig tree surrounded by brambles. I ascended the steps of the house, which had been worn smooth by untold generations of feet, and went inside.

Though time and weather had wreaked havoc with the house's exterior, the interior, though bare of furnishings, was intact. An entire wall of the kitchen was taken up with a huge fireplace flanked by baking chambers with iron doors in which bread had once baked. The whitewashed ceiling above the fireplace was still brown from the smoke and grease of cooking.

In the next room a thick vine had taken advantage of a broken window to grow inside. It clung to the ceiling, its rootlets penetrating the whitewash and plaster, leaving trails of white debris on the floor. The vine reached clear across the ceiling. Its leaves were ghostly pale for lack of light.

In one corner of the room stood a wooden chest whose every surface was carved with interlocking figures and geometric designs. Full of anticipation, I lifted the thick metal clasps, imagining a pirate's bounty of jewels and gold inside. Instead, I found a well-worn, rusty horseshoe.

I explored a few more houses and even found the village store and *kafeneon*. Most of the houses were in much worse shape than the first one I entered. Roofs had caved in everywhere and rock walls lay in ruinous heaps.

I aimed toward the church on the knoll, which had once been the center for the villagers who lived in the now silent and abandoned streets. But as I neared where the land rose to meet the church's door the way became so thick with brambles that I became entangled; thorns scratched my arms and brought blood. I gave up. The church had been the center of the villagers' existence. Perhaps now that the villagers were gone it was best if this center remained obscured and seen from a distance only, crumbling slowly under the hand of nature.

I walked to the edge of the village and climbed into the terraced fields so I could pick a route to the coast. Though I still couldn't see the coast I did see a stream that ran below the village, and I knew it would take the most direct route to the sea. I followed the contour of the land to where the stream dipped into a shallow ravine. There I turned to take one last look at the monastery, which loomed high on top of the rocky slope.

For so long I had been looking down into the scene I was about to enter; I had seen the road snaking along the coast toward Corfu Town like a ribbon of black rising and falling over the land's gentle undulations. I had seen Corfu Town itself, its white buildings changing hue in the light of the many-hued sun. I had watched boats docking and departing at the port, and I had watched as they slipped over the horizon toward Italy in the west and Patras on the Greek mainland in the south. I had watched the comings and goings of people on the island and I had seen the towns and villages in which they lived and worked. The whole while I had taken note, but not taken part. I had thought the thoughts of one in a clarified and more rarefied atmosphere. My feelings must have been close to those of William Butler Yeats when he wrote,

I have always sought to bring my mind close to the mind
of Indian and Japanese poets..., lay brothers whom I imagine

dreaming in some mediaeval monastery the dreams of their village, learned authors who refer all to antiquity; to immerse it in the general mind where that mind is scarce separable from what we have begun to call 'the subconscious'; to liberate it from all that comes of counsels and committees, from the world as it is seen from universities or populous towns…and [I] have put myself to school where all things are seen…

         ❧   ❧

Following the stream until the ravine became too narrow to continue, I climbed the riverbank. There I came upon a small trail. At first the size of an animal track, it quickly widened as it followed the slope of the mountain toward the coast. Soon I saw donkey tracks and knew I was nearing a village.

Rounding a corner, I came upon an elderly peasant woman clad in an old and patched dress. She was picking wild greens and stuffing them into a cloth sack. When she saw me her mouth gaped in toothless wonder at one the likes of me descending the mountain. She asked where I had come from.

"From the mountain," I said, "I came from the monastery. I live there."

Her face lit up. "You are a monk?"

"No, but I live with the monk who lives there."

"The monk is a very good man," she said as she tied the sack with a piece of rope. "He is generous and wise."

She threw the sack over her shoulder and walked with me down the path.

"You are not Greek," she said. "Your words come too slowly."

"I am from America."

"Ah, America! It is very good there, no?"

"Yes, it is; but it is good here too."

"Yes, it is good here," she said after thinking it over. "I have my house and my family. I have olive trees and a donkey, and I can pick greens. My life is good."

I saw that she was feeling the strain of the sack on her back. So I took it from her and put it over my shoulder. "Thank you," she said. "You are young and strong. I am old now. When you are old it is hard to carry heavy loads."

As we passed the first house at the edge of the village she called out to a woman sitting under a grape arbor surrounded by young children. "Anna, look what I've found! He's from America, and now he lives at the monastery on top of the mountain."

Anna came to take a better look. The children hid behind their mother's dress, giggling, peering out at me from time to time. Never addressing me directly, Anna asked the elderly woman some questions about me, and the old woman answered, beaming as if I were a new possession. As we took our leave, the children, who hadn't yet dared to say a word to me, called after us, "*Yassas, yassas,*" good-bye. They ran back to their veranda giggling the entire way.

Soon we came upon a low, whitewashed house surrounded by fruit trees. "This is my house," she said. "Come, I will give you coffee."

I deposited the sack of greens by the front door. She brought out a chair and put it in the shade of a mulberry tree. She told me to sit while she prepared the coffee. Soon an old man appeared at the door. He was bent with age and his face was deeply wrinkled. His whiskers were thick and long, almost like a cat's. He dragged a chair next to mine and letting out a long sigh, he sat. Then he said, "You are from America, no?"

"Yes, I am."

"Good, very good," then he stared through the olive grove on the other side of the dirt track as if he were trying to remember something. Then his eyes lit up and he raised his hand, forming it into a make-believe gun. "Bang-bang!" he said. "Chicago? No?"

His wife brought out a small table, covered it with a tablecloth, and carefully smoothed out the wrinkles. She then brought a tray with two small cups of Greek coffee, half a loaf of homemade bread, and a plate of olives and feta cheese. Occasionally someone passed the house, old women leading donkeys laden with sticks gathered on the mountain, or children returning from school in blue uniforms dirty from a day's wear.

"Look, he is from America," my hosts called to these passers-by. "We found him on the mountain!"

I finished my coffee in the shade of the mulberry tree then thanked them warmly for their hospitality. Promising to visit on my next trip down the mountain, I bid them good-bye. Then I walked down to the coast and hitched a ride to town.

The next morning I awoke to the sound of rain hitting my window at the Cyprus Hotel. Lingering over breakfast at the dairy shop, I hoped the rain would let up. It didn't. So at half past ten I started shopping—in the rain. I had stops to make all over town.

At the dry goods store I bought noodles, rice, beans, and—of course—chickpeas. At the butcher shop I bought a chicken and salted fish. Soon my pack was full, and my arms were full of bags.

At the vegetable shop, the old couple was glad to see me and asked about Andy and Ann. I told them about their return to London, and how I was living on the mountain. I took out my list and told the woman what I wanted: four kilos of potatoes, three of carrots, three of onions, and two of apples.

As I told her what I wanted a smile came to her face as if there was something to wonder at. I didn't understand what amazed her so, having only asked for some common vegetables.

Right then, another customer came into the shop, a woman I had seen there before. The proprietress turned to her. "This man," she said, "when he came to my shop a few weeks ago, he couldn't speak Greek. Now he speaks Greek!"

She gave me a big hug. The most amazing thing was that I understood every word she said.

The rain was falling so hard when I left the vegetable shop that I ducked into a *taverna* to have lunch and hopefully sit out the storm. I had only one more stop, at the wine merchant's shop, before catching the bus. But as I ate, the rain came even harder, and as I lingered over coffee the wind started to blow the rain horizontally. Since it was late, I had no choice but to brave the weather. Dodging puddles and resting under awnings, I made my way to the wine shop.

The wine merchant, a short and rather rotund man whose face was cast in a permanent grin, exuded a stench of wine every bit as strong as the large wooden casks that lined the walls of his shop. He noted my long absence then asked what he could do for me. I told him I wanted one jug of white wine and one jug of red. He asked me what kind. I told him inexpensive. Going to a shelf and rummaging through an assortment of spigots and jugs and the other paraphernalia of his trade, he presented me with two clay cups. He led me to a cask in the back room. The casks were made of bowed planks held together with metal rings. At the end of each was a hole, some of which were plugged with corks (the wine in these hadn't yet aged) and the others were tapped with spigots. Turning the spigot of the cask before us, he filled each of our cups. The dark red wine had the consistency and taste not only of the grapes from which it was made, but the very earth that produced them. He motioned that I was not merely to sip what was in my cup: I was to gulp it down. He brought me then to another cask where he refilled my cup with another dark red wine. This one was sweeter than the last but just as delicious. By the time I had quaffed it, he was refilling my cup with yet another vintage. My ears were beginning to ring and my head was feeling light. We sampled two more wines and it was all I could do to keep the shop from spinning.

He asked me which wine I liked best. Since the earthy taste of the first wine was so distinctive, I chose it. He told me I had chosen correctly; it was also his personal favorite. He filled a jug, put a cork in it, and said: "Now we must try the white wines."

He started filling my cup from a cask of white, and although I tried to tell him I would trust his judgment, he wouldn't hear of it. He insisted I try samples of quite a few. After a while I started spilling the wine behind a cask when he wasn't looking. Finally he asked me which I liked best. Although I couldn't remember how many I had tested or the differences between them, I chose the second.

His grin suddenly vanished. "But the first, *that* was a wine, *that* had body and flavor," he said. After an awkward moment, I assured him I had meant the first. Grin restored, he filled another jug.

Back in the front room of the shop I looked at the clock and realized that I had only ten minutes to get to the bus. Paying him quickly, I tried to pick up my load, but the jugs were just too much for me to carry along with the other sacks and bags, especially with the quantity of wine coursing through my veins. My attempt ended in everything tumbling to the floor. I began to panic. If I missed the bus I would have to spend two more days in Corfu waiting for the next bus. The monk needed food. I couldn't let him down.

Finally the wine merchant came to my rescue with some lengths of rope with which he tied the sacks together and lashed them to my pack. This left my hands free to carry the wine. I thanked him and ran from his shop into the deluge.

When I got to the bus square I was drenched, breathless, and sure I had missed the bus. But I searched anyway for the bus with the *Strinilas* destination card, and much to my surprise and great joy I found it. I jumped aboard and sat near the front with my over-laden pack and jugs of wine beside me. Immediately I heard a ripple of voices behind me. "*Filos tu papa,*" they were saying, Friend of the priest. I turned around and was met with many approving smiles.

As it turned out I needn't have worried about missing the bus, for the bus was going nowhere fast. We just sat there, everybody staring silently out the windows watching rain-drenched figures under umbrellas darting back and forth. The windows had fogged on the inside, so each stared through a tiny opening in the glass cleared with the back of the hand. Occasionally a bus would pass on its way out of the square, its engine roaring, the sound of tires plowing over drenched pavement, and the succession of uncomfortable wet people staring blankly through tiny cleared patches in fogged windows.

After half an hour I asked the man across from me what was going on. He told me that there were rumors from Strinilas that the road had washed out just below the village. But no one knew for sure. The driver was supposedly deciding whether to attempt it, but my neighbor suspected he was in a *kafeneon*, playing cards.

Then the driver got on the bus, stood in the front, and announced that the passengers headed for Episkepsis, a village on the other side of the mountains that was not as high as Strinilas, would be coming onto our bus. He would drive to Episkepsis first and if the road was good to that village he would attempt a trip higher into the mountains. Although some grumbled at this idea because it meant further delay, more driving, and only the possibility of reaching our destination, most kept their disapproval for the plan at bay. Our only hope was in humoring the driver. As the driver started the engine and awaited the arrival of the other passengers, an old woman hobbled up the aisle and gave him a piece of bread with some feta cheese on it. As she went back to her seat everyone patted her on the back and thanked her for her show of generosity on everyone's behalf. With this gesture came a deep sense of camaraderie among the passengers. Everyone began passing around loaves of bread and pieces of fruit. If we were to make it, it would be together. It was certain to be a long trip.

The passengers for Episkepsis arrived and I was pressed up against the window with my pack and bags on my lap and the jugs on the floor beneath my feet. Three other people sat on the seat that was meant for two, and that was the rule throughout the bus. The last people on had to stand. We were a single mass of pressed flesh.

The driver put the bus in gear and drove out of town and headed north along the coast road. The whole time my head was bent toward the window and locked in place by the man next to me whose arm was over my shoulders. Luckily my hand was just free enough to keep a little patch of the window clear in front of my eyes. Otherwise, I might have gone mad staring at the glass with beads of condensed human perspiration dripping down it.

When we arrived at the fork in the road where the way to Episkepsis went one way and the way to Strinilas the other, the bus stopped and the driver announced that all those headed for Strinilas would have to get off and wait for his return. The road to Episkepsis was a rough one, he explained, and he didn't want to go over it with such an over-crowded bus. And since he might not attempt to go up the mountain when he returned, he suggested that we look out for rides. He also asked us to get reports from anyone coming down the mountain about the condition of the road. Being made to stand out in the rain brought many protests, but in the end everyone headed for Strinilas got off the bus.

The driver had left us in a forsaken, desolate place. The clouds were low and in constant motion, alternately obscuring and revealing the steep rock faces that towered high overhead. The scene had the ethereal quality of a Chinese landscape painting in which different scenes on a single mountain are set apart by strange twists of perception created by layers of fog and mist. We were as one such scene on the scroll, a mass of humanity huddled under umbrellas surrounded by packages on a road that forked and became lost behind boulders and around turns, a road seemingly leading from nowhere to nowhere but simply existing within its own coordinates of time and place. The cliff over our heads was another such scene with its jagged rock face becoming occulted and softened by rounded wisps of cloud.

After half an hour a car came down the mountain. The driver said the road to Strinilas was in bad shape, especially for a bus, but if driven with care it was passable. This lightened our spirits, as did the sight of a goatherd coming around a bend in the road who invited us to take shelter in a little stone building not far from where we stood. Leaving a sentry to flag down the bus, the rest of us went with the goatherd. The building was just large enough to accommodate us all, and the thick straw on the floor was dry and comfortable to sit on. We were so wet and tired that we scarcely said a word until we heard the drone of the bus's engine coming up the road. We ran from the building *en masse* and were waiting for the bus when it stopped. We told the driver what the man in the car had said and he agreed to try it, although he did so grudgingly.

The road was bad, gouged by deep diagonal gullies and practically blocked in places by mudslides and fallen rock. Maneuvering around these obstacles proved dangerous, since to do so seemed always to entail passing within inches of a steep precipice, each of which was it-self undermined by the rain. At a dangerous turn of the road we came upon such a bad rockslide that it appeared our journey had ended. We could neither maneuver around the large rocks in the road nor pass over them. Since Strinilas was just a few miles away, the more hearty among us—myself included—decided to set out on foot. But when we were ready to go the old woman who had brought the bread and cheese to the driver announced that we either all go or none of us go. "And since I am too old to walk that far," she said, "the only solution is that we clear the road!" Enthusiasm for her idea spread quickly, and within seconds everyone was on the road removing rocks according to his or her ability, the very young and old picking up little rocks and throwing them to the side while those of strength and agility banded together and rolled the large boulders out of the way. The entire while the old woman moved amongst us, offering encouragement and advice. She was a grand ma-triarch and road commissioner in one. Within minutes we had cleared a wide enough aisle for the bus to pass through. We reached Strinilas without further incident.

Chapter 16

When the bus stopped in the village everybody scattered for their houses, leaving me alone in the heavy rain, feeling wet and forlorn. Hoisting the pack and looping the bags of food through my arms, I threw my poncho over my shoulders and picked up the two jugs of wine. The road that led through the village was deserted except for a few wet dogs curled up together in a doorway, shivering in their sleep. The wind howled, ballooning the poncho behind me.

When I reached the last stone house of the village, whose back door opened to the mountain's wild, untamed slope, an old woman came running out to me. She stood before me in the rain, her face wrinkled and her eyes large and soft with compassion. Her dress was the color of the earth; her apron had flour on it. She stared at me, taking stock of my situation. Then she pointed toward the mountain and said, "*Epáno?*" Up? I said yes, and she muttered something beneath her breath. A look of consternation crossed her face as if it were she who was going up. She wanted to relieve me of my suffering and discomfort by taking them upon herself, as we stood frozen in time with wisps of fog enveloping us. She held out her hand, caught some drops of rain, and said, "*Vroní,*" rain. I nodded. Another moment passed. She turned. She took a few steps; then she stopped to see if I was really going *epáno*. Seeing I was, she crossed herself and scurried to the shelter of her house, leaving me alone to face the mountain.

By the time I reached the dirt track that led to the monastery, the wind had risen to a ferocious howl. As I climbed the trail I entered the low clouds. This was the point of no return: I could still turn back—

surely the woman at that last house would put me up—but if I continued I'd have to reach the top. Although the wind blew right through me, I heard no thunder; nor did I see flashes of lightning. Uncorking the bottle of white wine, I took some large gulps, and with renewed confidence pushed on through the boulder-strewn landscape. I prayed that the monk was at the lower monastery, and that there would be a fire and supper waiting for me when I arrived. I could just see the kitchen suffused with the fire's warm glow.

But that was all in my mind's eye. What I actually saw I took at first for an apparition. In the gathering darkness, two dark figures emerged from the thick fog. It was beyond my wildest imaginings that I would encounter others where I myself felt like a stranger amid the forces of nature. Panic seized me. I slipped quietly behind a huge boulder. Their wavering forms quickly took shape: one was short and stout and bent almost double against the wind, and the other, taller and more erect, was wearing a long robe that billowed in the gusting wind. It was the monk and a man from the village.

I jumped out from my hiding place, causing both of them to gasp in fright.

"Thomás," the monk yelled, "eh, Thomás!"

Then he said, "A woman in the village has died. I must go to the church. The lower monastery is locked. Go to the upper monastery. I will meet you there in a few days. May God be with you! The storm is raging upon the mountain!"

And with that he was gone. He didn't even stop to tell me the news. He told me in passing, as he and the villager continued toward the safety of the village. I stood watching the two men dissolve into the darkening night, taking with them all hope of a warm fire at the end of my journey. Instead of the monk cooking the chicken while I warmed myself before the fire, I now saw the cool and damp bed that awaited me. I cursed it all. "Eh, Thomás," I said aloud, donning the monk's raspy voice, "you are a crazy man!"

Ahead of me was nothing but storm and fog-obscured mountain. Putting my hands out before me, I touched the soft limits of what I could discern. The fog deepened. Opacity turned to night.

Nothing of what I knew would be of help here. Darkness had descended. I was alone with the mountain. Much of who I was fell away at that moment. I was both closer to the animal and to the divine. My senses sharpened. Into me flowed the raw forces of nature. The mountain stood solid and unmoving—a mass of bare rock forced to the sky, pounded by rough weather. The air was thick with cloud and cold. Rain was falling heavily now. Everywhere rivulets flowed and merged together. Distant rumblings of thunder sharpened my awareness to a keen edge, and in the distance through the rain-filled fog dim flashes reached my eyes.

I felt strong, as if I too were an element along with mountain, cloud, rain, and lightning. We had all existed before in this heightened tension of warring elements. And strange as it may sound, I now felt completely at home so far from anything human. I came to know myself in elemental simplicity as the warring forces called me into their sphere.

I felt myself as one with every human being who has gone to the edge of the earth, to the bottom of the ocean, or to the roof of the world. My steps were their steps; we walked in a timeless moment of interpenetration.

The thunder came closer and the lightning became more intense. But I was not afraid. I was behind myself, watching my eyes watch the world, hearing my ears listen to the whirl of the wind, and feeling my body weak from the cold and the weight of my load. I felt what Thomas felt, saw what he saw, and heard what he heard; yet I was behind it all, unmoved and unconcerned.

I would have felt with equal indifference if lightning had struck a tree on the slopes or a rock on the path, smashing it to pieces; I would have felt the same if it had been me who had been struck. It would have mattered little. Would the winds have ceased to howl? Would the rain have ceased to lash? Or how about the mountain: would it cease to expose its rocky face to the pounding elements?

I was walking up a barren mountain road, yet I didn't know how long I'd been on it. As I progressed from one turn of the road to the next, I felt like the sailor whose boat is being dashed by the storm: he cares little of his final destination. The trough of one wave and the crest of the next is as far as his senses will take him

Finally, I heard the clanging of a bell and knew its sound as a fledgling bird knows its mother's call. It was the bell above the monastery gate being rung by the wind. I went through the gate with the sense of relief that a sailor feels when his storm-racked boat comes in sight of land, and he recognizes it as his own harbor as he glides in through the well-known channel, knowing that his feet will soon touch solid earth. I opened the door to my little room, dumped the food and wine on the floor, and lay on the bed, falling instantly into a deep sleep.

Chapter 17

The next morning I awoke from a dream that had the clarity of a vision and the immediacy of waking life. Sometimes a dream stands out like a clear signpost on a dark roadway. One drives one's car along these dark roadways every night and occasionally the headlights fall on something significant. Usually the headlights are dim, the messages obscure. It is the intensity of the beam that determines the clarity of the vision. And one can never be too sure. One never knows the origin of a dream. As the wise Penelope, wife of Odysseus, said,

> Dreams, sir, are awkward and confusing things: not all that people see in them comes true. For there are two gates through which these insubstantial visions reach us, one is of horn and the other of ivory. Those that come through the ivory gate cheat us with empty promises that never see fulfillment; while those that issue from the gates of burnished horn inform the dreamer what will really happen.

Occasionally one has a dream whose place of issue is clear, a dream that leaves behind a deep sense of a destiny, a potential to be fulfilled. This was just such a dream. Dreams like this reflect the deeper patterns of which we ourselves are but reflections.

I dreamed I was sitting at the desk in my cell surrounded by papers and piles of open books. I was writing in a blue notebook. Then a voice rang in my ears. It was an ancient voice, the voice of someone as old as time itself, a voice more familiar even than my own. It was the voice of the Mother, not *my* mother—though her voice was reflected in it; this was a far more ancient voice, that of the Great Mother, the matrix of all.

She said to me, "Go look under the tree."

So I opened the door and there, where the stunted trees had always stood in the middle of the courtyard, stood a colossal tree, a tree whose branches swept the clouds and whose trunk would have taken thirty people to encompass. At the base of its great trunk, where its ancient roots twisted and turned along the ground before delving down to the very foundation of the mountain itself, was a fish. I bent down and picked up the fish.

Then I was plunged into darkness. I could no longer see what I held in my hands, so I looked at it under a quick succession of lights of increasing intensity, beginning with a match, then a candle, then a lantern, then an electric light, until it was by the light of the sun itself that I was looking at it.

The scene changed and I was bringing the fish to the house where the Great Mother lived. She greeted me at the door clad in a flowing white robe. She was pleased I had recognized her voice and had carried out her instructions. She took the fish and went inside. A moment later she reappeared, holding out a goblet filled with a chalky white mixture she had made from the fish.

"Drink this," she said. "It will bring you good luck in your upcoming travels."

I drank it and woke up.

Opening the door to brilliant Greek sunshine, I saw that the violent storm of the previous evening had passed, leaving the air crisp and clear. I walked to the low wall beyond the kitchen and looked down over the slopes of the mountain.

The clarity with which I looked at the mountain was not a result merely of the clean air. For the first time I was seeing the mountain for what it was, in itself. Always before my view of the mountain had been tainted by my own personal stamp. I had always been preoccupied with myself when I had looked at it. It took the storm of the previous day to shake me loose from that preoccupation, to be prepared to be struck down like a pine along its slopes. A subtle yet powerful shift had occurred in my center of gravity.

Something new flowed inside me, as if I had lifted a rock to allow a clear spring to gush forth. But this spring was not new. It had flowed before, deep in my past; and it flowed before any past I could call my own. It was far more ancient than that. It was as old and familiar as the Mother of my dream. I was gazing over the mountain with the fresh and immediate clarity and wonder I had experienced as a child.

And with this clarity came a feeling of fruition, as if something was complete. Every particular fit in place and the patterns they created merged with the universal. Each moment in time stood perfected, lacking nothing from the past and yearning for nothing in the future.

Then the wheels turned again; time moved a notch and there was something to be fulfilled. Like an undertow coming suddenly at the changing of the tide, I knew my time on the mountain would be drawing to a close. The words of the Mother came ringing to my ears, "Drink this," she had said, "it will bring you good luck in your upcoming travels."

From the top of the mountain I could sense the roundness of the earth implicit in the encircling horizon. The horizon seemed not that far away, and the earth itself seemed rather small. I wondered which point on the horizon hid my next destination.

I looked south, past the island's southern tip, toward Crete. Crete would be warm. I could speak Greek there and still be with Greeks, of whom I had grown so fond. Beyond Crete lay Egypt and the rest of Africa, a whole continent of deserts, plains, and jungles, whose villages and towns were populated with people who spoke languages as strange and alien as Greek had been when I first arrived. I knew I could learn one of these languages, and I knew these people could become my friends. Then I looked east. Beyond the Albanian mountains—across Turkey, Persia, Afghanistan, and Pakistan—was India, whose ancient cultural and spiritual traditions had long drawn me to them. Intuition seemed to confirm the unity that the Eastern thinker sees behind the multiplicity of the phenomenal world. I thought perhaps it was to their land that my steps would tend. In the west was Europe. I had long wanted to go to Assisi, the town in Italy where Saint Francis had lived. And beyond Europe, across the ocean, were my family and friends. I thought of the soft rolling hills of Vermont and I knew I would return there one day. I knew my travels would circle back to their beginnings, but I also knew the circle was only partially complete.

It was an intuition that first brought me to the mountain Pantokrator, and if that had taught me anything it was that conscious intentions don't always lead to the goal. The traveler leaves the known world—as well as all pre-conceived notions—behind, and opens himself to the world of chance. He takes a step into the world's flux. He must enter the flow and follow it.

Since I had to leave Greece—if only to step foot in another country to receive a new visa—I decided to take the boat to Italy, which was the closest foreign landfall. Once I arrived there I could decide what to do next.

I decided to leave the mountain on a Tuesday, two days before the monk had to go to Corfu Town for his monthly meeting with the other priests and monks on the island. We arranged to meet in a *taverna* in town for an early lunch before my ferry left. This made it easier to leave the monastery since I only had to bid the monastery and mountain good-bye. I would be seeing the man again. And having a full day on the coast would allow me plenty of time to return my books to the Anglican Church library, go to Kontókali to bid my old neighbors good-bye, and take one last stroll through Corfu Town.

On the day of my departure I awoke before dawn and watched the sun rise over the Albanian mountains one last time. Then I spent hours walking around the courtyard and sitting on boulders outside the monastery gate trying to etch into memory every sight, smell, and sound of the place. When it was time for me to go, the monk brought me to the church and he lit a candle for my safe journey. We stood in front of the burning candle in an attitude of prayer with our eyes closed for some time. Then I walked down the switchbacking road under the same heavy load of clothing and books as when I arrived. I turned when I reached the lower monastery and saw the monk's black form above the monastery wall. He raised his arms and waved good-bye to me. I waved back, turned, and continued across the gray plateau without a backward glance.

Thursday morning I arrived at the *taverna* early, sat on a chair outside the front door, and awaited the monk's arrival. I first spied him some distance down the road. He was wearing a new robe. It wasn't the patched one he wore at the monastery, but one he must have kept packed away for these occasional trips to town. His progress down the road was slow, for everybody seemed to know him, and when they stopped to speak with him they showed him great reverence, a reverence that seemed deeper and more heart-felt than I had seen shown toward other priests and monks.

When he arrived, we sat at a table and ordered our meals and some beer. The food came quickly. We ate in an awkward silence, both feeling the sadness of parting.

When we had finished eating the monk broke the silence. "Thomás, one day you come back. You bring your wife and your children and you all stay with me. I will still be on the mountain. You will travel by boat, plane, and train to see the world and I will see it from the mountain Pantokrator. It is not so different in the end. But remember, when you come back I will be an old man. I will have a cane and I will hobble from place to place."

"But my friend," I said, "I will always be able to recognize you. No matter how old you are you will always be the one with fire in his eyes!" Then we laughed our last laugh together.

We stood to leave and hugged one another with lumps growing in our throats. Then we faced each other in an awkward silence, neither of us knowing what to say. He turned and made for the door as fast as he could.

Just as he was about to step outside I yelled out in English, "Good-bye, you sly chickpea!"

He whipped around with his finger to his mouth, his eyes scanning the *taverna* to see if anyone else had heard, which of course they had for I had yelled it out, and they were all staring at us.

Then he realized I had spoken in English and no one else understood my words. It had been our little secret and it would remain so. Then, forgetting the presence of the others, he shook his finger at me as he had so many times in front of the crackling fire, and he said, "Eh, *Thomás!*"

ॐ   ॐ

Then I was on the ferryboat to Italy, leaning against the stern rail, watching the Island of Corfu recede behind the boat. Instead of fading out of view, it remained clear till the very end when it suddenly sank beneath the horizon. The earth's curvature had claimed it. The last thing I saw was the high cone of the mountain Pantokrator.

Postscript

I returned to Corfu in 2002, twenty years after my time on Mount Pantokrator with the monk Evdókimos. I had stopped off on the island especially to see him, expecting to stay a few days before flying on to India. But a mistake by a travel agent invalidated my flight reservation, and the next available seat wasn't for an entire month. So I suddenly had a month on my hands. Greece was not as I remembered it. The Euro had just been introduced, and prices had soared. First I went to Kontókali to see the house where I had lived with Andy and Ann. But I couldn't find it. I wasn't even sure I was looking on the right hillside. Kontókali was full of huge hotels and a big marina, and it was even difficult to say where the original village was.

When I got to Corfu Town I went straight to a bakery run by people from Strinilas, Evdókimos' village at the base of the mountain. I asked them how he was. I didn't even know if he was still alive.

They told me he was well, but that he was no longer on the mountain. My Greek was so rusty and their English so rudimentary that I couldn't figure out why. But I was stunned by the news. His leaving the mountain seemed as improbable as the monastery itself relocating. After so many years on the mountain he was practically synonymous with it. He had lived there so long that he resembled it. It was in his blood. Where else could he possibly live?

They told me he was living right there in Corfu Town and could be found at a monastery not far from the hospital. They explained how to find it. On my way I stopped at a grain dealer and pinched a single chickpea from an open sack.

Evthókimos Koskinás with the author, 2002

Evdókimos' new monastery was right in town, not far from the center. I walked into the courtyard just as a black-robed monk with his back to me was locking the door of the monastery chapel. He turned around and it was Evdókimos, older of course, but it was him. He came down the stairs and I strode right up to him. I knew he wouldn't recognize me. It had been twenty years. I used to have a beard. He stopped, wondering what I wanted. I motioned that he should hold out his hand so I could put something into it. He hesitated, knitted his thick bushy white eyebrows, and looked at me. Then curiosity got the better of him and he held his hand out, palm up. I placed the chickpea in the center of his palm. He looked at it, then looked at me in puzzlement—wondering, no doubt, what this crazy foreigner wanted with him. Then he looked again at the chickpea and the sudden recognition practically knocked him off his feet.

"Thomas!!" he exploded, and he embraced me with such force that I practically fell. He grabbed me by the arm and brought me inside to where his brother monks were drinking coffee in a small whitewashed room with big windows. Patting my back with tremendous force, he told them how I had lived on the mountain with him, and now had returned out of the blue after twenty years. I had thought perhaps he had left the mountain because of his advanced age or because of failing health, but this obviously couldn't be. He brimmed with vitality.

When I told him I suddenly had a month to wait, and that I had been hoping to find him on the mountain, he hesitated not a moment in inviting me to stay with him in town. So I did. He lived now in his own apartment in Corfu Town about a ten minute walk from his new monastery. It was strange seeing him in this new context, dodging cars instead of lightning bolts. He had a tiny apartment on the third floor, a small living-room-cum-bedroom, and a kitchen. I slept in the kitchen on a fold-out cot. The kitchen was so small that when I set out my bed, there was hardly room to put my feet on the ground. I was apprehensive at first about sharing such a small space with him, especially since we hadn't seen each other in twenty years. But it was like old times, even though the sound through the walls was from the neighbors instead the whistling wind, laden with cloud.

On the mountain, Evdókimos had taught me passable Greek in a surprisingly short time. Twenty years later, only the rudiments remained. It took some time, but I did learn why he left the mountain, and it was not of his own volition. The Orthodox Church of Corfu got a new bishop who thought more of money than the sanctity of Church property or preserving the monastery as a place of solitude and prayer. It apparently didn't cause him the slightest pang of conscience to turn the monastery into a money maker, even if it meant kicking out the monk who had lived in the mountaintop monastery for 54 years. The Bishop only had eyes for the monastery's potential, and what a gold mine it could be, the tourist shops that could be installed in the courtyard, the tourists who would be attracted by such a spectacular setting. When I heard of this unconscionable act, I practically cried. Evdókimos had moved up there from Strinilas when he was 23 years old and had lived there until he was 77.

Evdókimos hit the nail right on the head when he first told me what happened. He rubbed his fingers together, his wild gray eyebrows trembling with simmering fury, one eye locked on me while the other hovered over my right shoulder. "Hrimata, Thomas. Hrimata!" he said. Hrimata means money. As he repeated this word, his foot came out from under his robe and he kicked the air as if kicking the new bishop in the ass.

Since my Greek was pretty rusty, the clearest explanation I got for what happened came from a local magazine, in an article entitled *The Monk of Pantokrator*:

> Since the war, for many decades the monastery was in the sole charge of the monk Evdokimos Koskinas, who acted as unpaid abbot, caring for it with untold devotion and diligence. He would celebrate mass every day invariably alone. He delighted in his peaceful and simple life in solitude, meditation and prayer, greatly enjoying showing visitors around. The monastery was his pride and joy, his home and his castle.

Then, one day in 1998, the newly appointed Bishop of Corfu, Timotheos, paid a visit. On leaving Pantokrator, he reckoned, "there's gold in that there mountain". Accordingly, he ordained that a gift shop should be installed inside the monastery for the sale of religious symbols, postcards, cigarettes, ice-cream and the usual tourist trash displayed on stalls throughout the island. Evdokimos, supported by all the local villagers, raised serious objections, pointing out that such a venture was sacrilege in a place which had been consecrated and that there were empty monks' cells outside which would serve the purpose. A petition was then drawn up, bearing hundreds of signatures, and presented to the bishop, who simply gave two episcopal fingers to the protesters and the project went ahead. This prompted Evdokimos to take a leaf out of the 21st chapter of St Mark's Gospel with the paraphrased rebuke, 'This monastery is a place of prayer - ye hath made it a den of commerce." Whereupon the saintly monk divested himself of his religious robes, vowed he would serve no more and went into 'retreat'.[1]

Evdókimos was persuaded somehow to take back his robes and join the monastery in town where, the article concluded, "...at the going down of the sun, Evdokimos can be spotted tolling the knell of parting day, doubtless reflecting with nostalgia on the halcyon days of yore."

A few days after I arrived, Evdókimos' nephew drove the two of us to the monastery so I could see it. Later I wished I had left my last impression of the place intact. A proper road now snaked across the moon-like plateau and switchbacked up the final cone of the mountain to the monastery. This road was bisected by others, which senselessly scarred the surrounding mountains. And there were metal road signs everywhere—all in the name of tourist development.

---

1   Island Magazine, Issue 9, Winter 2008, pg. 41

From afar the monastery itself was dwarfed by dozens of new communications towers, huge dishes relaying radio waves and microwaves from Corfu Town to the mainland. There were TV and radio transmission towers, mobile phone relay stations, and an array of strange-looking wires and antennas. The road ended at a parking lot for tourists. The front gate of the monastery was still the same, with the two bells that used to ring by themselves in a gale. But to the right of the gate they had constructed a restaurant and bar, which also sold trinkets and post cards. Outside was a pay telephone. Tourists were milling about.

Evdókimos stayed at the car and refused to go near the gate. I think he was afraid that if I they saw me with him, they wouldn't let me enter. "If you want to go, go look alone," he said. He had had a tussle with the monks who now ran the place. He didn't want to see them, and besides it was just too painful for him to see what they'd done.

The gate was locked. I looked through a crack and saw that the courtyard had been laid with stone walkways, gardens, and benches for tourists. I was glad I couldn't see the gift shops. The interior of the monastery is still intact in my memory.

When I returned to the car, the wind that billowed the monk's black robe was the same. Everything else had changed.

We soon fell into a routine based on Evdókimos' schedule at the monastery. He would leave for the monastery early, before six, to pray and perform his duties there. Sometimes I would hear him leave, but usually I'd sleep through. I'd awaken at a reasonable hour, have a simple breakfast of bread, honey, and coffee, and often spent the morning writing, doing laundry, or shopping for food. Evdókimos would come home in the early afternoon, after eating lunch at the monastery, and he would take a nap. Then he'd return to the monastery in the late afternoon, and I usually took a walk into town and sit on the battlements of the Old Fort overlooking the water and read or just look out at the waves and birds gliding over the water.

As on the mountain, Evdókimos insisted on cooking, and we'd have wonderful meals drenched in olive oil and spiced with garlic, oregano, and thyme. I'd do the dishes, then we'd settle down together at his table for the evening. These were like the evenings at the monastery except that instead of being bathed in the flickering light of a wood fire, he'd put the TV on, and we'd sit there in its glow. He had a small leather-bound copy of the Gospels. With reading glasses on he'd follow the words with his finger, his lips mouthing out the words, and I'd sit on the other side of the table with my notebook and pen, writing, often describing the scene as it unfolded. He'd keep half an eye on his Bible, half on the TV, like he used to on the mountain when tending the fire. Instead of the metal poker, he had the remote, and he often switched stations. Sometimes we'd talk, but mostly we'd sit in a comfortable silence; the TV was turned so low I doubt he could follow what the people said. It was about as loud as the hissing of the wet wood in a fire on a stormy night in the monastery fireplace.

Occasionally he'd comment about something on TV. I'd be writing. "Thomas," he'd say. I'd look up and he'd nod toward the TV, like the time there was an exposé on some black-leather devil worshippers in Holland. "Kako," he said gravely, shaking his head. "Kako." Bad.

A few days into this routine he called my name and indicated that I should look at the TV. There was an advertisement for a car with a scantily dressed young woman provocatively running her hand along its smooth lines. I thought for sure he wanted to show me something that had been interrupted by the ad. It was slightly embarrassing to be looking at half naked woman in his presence. But when I looked back he was smiling at me with a smile I'd never seen before on his face. He raised his bushy eyebrows in some sort of male comradery—but I was sure I was misreading it. I went back to my writing and he went back to his Gospel.

The next night something similar happened. This time it was a Greek soap opera. He called my attention to the TV just as a man with his tie undone and a glamorous woman in a slinky black dress were entering a bedroom, obviously intent on ripping each other's clothes off and making wild love. "Man, Woman," he said in Greek. Then he made a gesture with his hands that I can only describe as imitating mating rabbits. It was an innocent gesture, like a young boy might make. He tried to catch my eye, raising his eyebrow significantly, but I averted my gaze and pretended to read over what I'd just been writing. I was sure I was somehow misreading him, yet I didn't dare look up. He was a monk. He was 80 years old.

Night after night, a similar scene was repeated until he asked me a question I never thought I'd hear coming from those old lips, and it wasn't only because he asked it in English.

"Sex Good?" he asked.

What could I say?

"Yes," I said, "Sex Good."

He got visibly excited by my answer. Then he asked how many women I'd made love to in my life. Thugh I understood his question, I pretended not to and went back to writing. Then he asked me how old I was when I first made love to a woman. I dodged his question by pretending I didn't understand and telling him how old I was. "I am 43 years old," I said. "No," he said, and he repeated his question. I responded by saying, "You are 81, I am 43." He went back to his Gospel with one eye on the TV.

This went on for some nights. He'd spent most of his life in his mountain retreat dressed in the black robe that insured women covered themselves and acted chaste in his presence. Now he was bombarded with blatantly sexual images every evening. And though he wore that black robe, he was still a man. It would have been unthinkable for him to ask a Greek about sex. I was an outsider, and a trusted outsider, the only one he knew, so I provided the only possible chance he had to speak with another human being about so basic a human experience—one he'd been denied. So after quite a few days of dodging his questions, I decided to tell him, in my broken Greek, what he wanted to know. So the next time he asked me about sex, I answered him. It was all pretty basic, that it felt good, how old I was the first time, things like that. When I told him that it made you feel close to the woman, he nodded his head vigorously, like he knew what I was saying was true. I think he even grunted. He, who had never made love, was having his first man-to-man talk in his life. It must have been so pent up inside him, never being able to broach the subject, that he started trembling with excitement. His right eyebrow started twitching with a nervous tick. He must have wanted to speak with someone about this for the sixty years of his monkhood. He told me he had never touched a woman in his entire life. He held up his Bible when he told me this, and I didn't doubt him for a moment. He was a true monk. It was a life that fulfilled him and gave him tremendous depth. Yet having denied himself the company of women for so long, he was still a man with the feelings we all share. I don't think he regretted the vow he had taken as a young man, but he was curious, he needed to know. It made him even more human. In the end I was honored he asked me. It was really quite moving.

When the time was coming for me to leave the island, Evdókimos brought out a large photo book on Mount Athos, the peninsula in Macedonia in northern Greece which has been autonomous under the Patriarch of Constantinople since Byzantine times and upon which are twenty monasteries of the various Orthodox countries. Known as the Holy Mount, it is forbidden for women or children to set foot on the peninsula. It is a World Heritage site recognized by UNESCO. He showed me photographs of the Pantokrator Monastery on Mount Athos. He patted me on the shoulder with his powerful hand and said, "Thomas, Evdókimos—one day, we go Mount Athos!" I don't think he had ever been there. I was honored he was inviting me to go with him to this supreme pilgrimage place of the Orthodox world. He told me not to wait too long, for he was old now and would soon be unable to make such an arduous journey.

When he brought me to the boat when I was leaving the island, he gave me a tremendous hug. He had a tear in his eye as he turned and walked quickly away. I had a lump in my throat. We never made that pilgrimage to Mount Athos. In the process of writing this Postscript, I learned that after a short illness he died peacefully on August 7, 2011 at the age of 90 and was buried in Corfu Town.

ABOUT THE AUTHOR

Writer and photographer Thomas K. Shor was born in Boston, USA, and studied comparative religion and literature in Vermont. With an ear for unusual stories, the fortune to attract them and an eye for detail, he has travelled the planet's mountainous realms—from the Mayan Highlands of southern Mexico in the midst of insurrection to the mountains of Greece and, more recently to the Indian Himalayas—to collect, illustrate and write stories with a uniquely personal character, often having the flavor of fable.

Shor has lectured widely on his writings and has had solo exhibits of his photographs in Europe and in India. He can often be found in the most obscure locales, immersed in a compelling story touching upon fundamental human themes.

Vistit him at:
www.ThomasShor.com

ALSO BY THOMAS K. SHOR

A STEP AWAY FROM PARADISE

A Tibetan Lama's Extraordinary Journey
to a Land of Immortality

Penguin Books, 2011
City Lion Press, 2017

IN THE EARLY 1960s, a Tibetan lama, a charismatic and learned visionary mystic named Tulshuk Lingpa, led over 300 followers into the high glaciers of the Himalayas in order to 'open the way' to a hidden land of immortality fabled in Tibetan tradition dating back at least to the 12th century.

Fifty years later, Thomas K. Shor tracks down the surviving members of this visionary expedition and entwines their remarkable stories of faith and adventure with his own quest to discover the reality of this land known as Beyul. What emerges is a breathtaking story alive with possibility, bringing the reader as close to the Hidden Land as a book possibly can. As the astounding account unfolds, the reader is sure to repeat the question constantly raised by the author in his interviews: And then what happened?

A STEP AWAY FROM PARADISE tells the story of Lama Tulshuk Lingpa's life and his unlikely expedition to a land beyond cares while reflecting on what this means for the rest of us. It draws on both research and extensive interviews with his surviving disciples and family members. The book is richly illustrated with portraits of those who went with Tulshuk Lingpa and the places he traveled to. The book also delves into the tradition within Tibetan Buddhism of Shambhala and the hidden valleys, which mirror legends around the world of utopias and lands of milk and honey, thus showing that the quest for the hidden land is a universal urge of humanity.

A STEP AWAY FROM PARADISE is a riveting tale of adventure, intrigue and Devotion. [It] deals with an aspect of Tibetan Buddhism that is in some ways more honest to the real spirit of Tibet than all the usual books on Tibetan doctrine and will, I am sure, be of interest to a wide audience. It is a fascinating account of a little-known charismatic figure that will challenge even the most skeptical mind and provide a fresh perspective on what we normally regard as 'reality.'

Like no other book I have ever read, A STEP AWAY FROM PARADISE is both unique and intriguing. Highly recommended.

INTO THE HANDS
OF THE UNKNOWN

An Indian Sojourn with a Harvard Renunciant

Escape Media Publishers, 2003
Pilgrim Publishers, 2006
City Lion Press, 2019

"I think you should come with me to India"

Thus begins the story of the author at the age of 21, when he happened to sit next to Ed Spencer, a brilliant 70-year-old ex-Harvard professor turned wandering holy man, who makes this offer within an hour of their meeting on a Greek ferry.

Though unsure whether the old man is some kind of a bum or a realized being or both, he agrees to go with this enigmatic stranger whose credo is: "Take the money out of your pocket and put yourself in the hands of the Unknown."

When they arrive at the border and Ed passes the money exchange with hardly a glance, Shor begins to understand the gulf that separates the old man from the rest of humanity.

The ensuing journey takes us on an epic trip by foot into the heart of South India and then to the Himalayas where the author makes his first contact with the Tibetan people.

Into the Hands of the Unknown has been revised and has a new Postscript describing Shor's subsequent encounters with Ed Spencer. The book was originally published as Part II of Windblown

FROM THE REVIEW BY THE RENOWNED
BRITISH POET KATHLEEN RAINE

In Thomas Shor's narrative the absorbing writing is the least of his gifts: he creates the imaginative adventure of his life as he lives it.

Thomas Shor's life is a continual unfolding of those inner and outer worlds which his sense of wonder discovers continually. His story reminds us that we are, or could be, travelers in a world of marvels, of love, and encounters with men and women themselves on pilgrimages of the imagination. Did not the Emperor Haroun al-Rashid for a thousand and one nights hear in the city of Baghdad endless stories that make up the one story of the world? Once involved in Thomas Shor's adventure of life, one hopes only for more.

~Kathleen Raine (D.Litt., Cambridge; Commander of the Ordre des Arts et des Lettres, France; Commander of the British Empire; Winner—Queen's Gold Medal for Poetry, England, etc.)

THE MASTER DIRECTOR

A Journey through Politics, Doubt and Devotion

with a Himalayan Master

HarperCollins, 2014

"Maybe you shouldn't go back to Darjeeling. It
might not be safe for you…"
The lama was in the next room. It was 2 a.m.
He was trying to calm his attendants. I think the
boys wanted to kill me.
This was my last day with Gurudev.

In this riveting true story, Thomas K. Shor, an adventuring American
writer with an ear for unusual stories, has no idea what he is getting into
when he wanders into a Sikkimese mountain village and into the life of
an enigmatic spiritual master known as Gurudev.

As Gurudev, a Tibetan Buddhist lama, lavishes the author with pres-
ents and invites him into his inner circle—thereby offering him, and us, a
unique glimpse into a master's life and his teachings of universal love—it
seems destiny is at work. But what happens when it turns out the master
has close ties with the local dictator and his henchmen and Shor finds
himself staying with the lama at their houses? How is he to reconcile the
religion of love with the violence of politics? Gurudev's 'engaged Buddhism' not only stretches common notions of morality, but also spins
Shor's moral compass. Ultimately, the author flees Darjeeling under
physical threat and abandons the writing of this book—until now.

The Master Director, richly illustrated with over 75 photos, probes
the limits of charisma and skepticism, doubt, and devotion. And throughout, Shor's captivating story treads the fine line of openness without
credulity, and questioning without prejudice. While the warnings are
many against mixing religion and politics, they combine in this enter-
taining tale set in the politically tumultuous foothills of India's eastern
Himalayas to reveal profound insights into the nature of both the human
and the divine.

LEOPARD IN THE CITY

An Urban Fable

City Lion Press, 2018

A Leopard is Loose in the City!

LEOPARD IN THE CITY tells the tale of a leopard, a real leopard of the jungle, who suddenly finds himself in the center of a huge European city.

If seen, even by a single human being, he knows his fate would be sealed—either with a bullet through his heart or the sting of a tranquilizer gun, followed by a lifetime behind bars at the city zoo.

And who's to say which would be worse? In the zoo he would live out his days being gawked at as an anomaly, the famous mystery leopard from who-knows-where, the wild beast everybody read about in the newspapers, the one who disrupted life in the city and then was caught.

What he really needs is a miracle.

In order to avoid detection, he only moves about in the shadows deep in the night. Finding no edge to the city, no place where the city ends and the jungle begins, he sets himself the task of learning the ways of human beings. By understanding them he hopes to discover a loophole, a way out.

Befriended by a house cat, he comes to understand that long before human beings domesticated cats and dogs, they domesticated themselves: they tamed their own wild natures. It was by harnessing themselves that they were then able to harness nature's laws, which led ultimately to the engineering of skyscrapers and the angled grid of streets which appear to have no end, and through which the leopard is now forced to navigate.

Should he give up the dream of escape and follow the path of domestication as laid out by house cats, whose ancestors sacrificed their wild natures for security? Is it true, as house cats would have it, that the way to freedom is to submit willingly to domestication? Does way to salvation really lie in captivity? Does freedom come from in accepting subjugation? Is safety truly found not in liberty, but in the confinement, in the comfortable fate of a house cat living a privileged life of leisure with a secure place by the fire?

SCULPTURE GARDEN
OF THE GODS

ANIMATED LANDSCAPE PHOTOGRAPHY
FROM THE GREEK ISLAND OF IKARIA

City Lion Press, 2018

The Greek island of Ikaria has gained notoriety lately for being a so-called "Blue Zone," one of the select places on the planet where people live the longest. This otherwise obscure island was also known to the Ancients as the birthplace of the Greek god of ecstasy and wine, Dionysus, who was born upon the rocky ridge of mountain that runs down the center of the island.

SCULPTURE GARDEN OF THE GODS, a book of black and white photographs and prose, is the fruit of the author's three winters upon this mountain—often blown by hurricane-force winds and engulfed in thick fog.

Shor weaves the poetic force of his eye with that of his pen to take us on a journey to this otherworldly landscape, where lashing winds sculpt solid granite into forms that look like living beings with an uncanny regularity.

It is a place of mystery and beauty, where the most enduring is dissolved by the most fleeting, where wisps of fog blown by a gale can cause an entire mountain-side to disappear in an instant.

GANGES LAMENT

BLACK & WHITE PHOTOGRAPHIC PORTRAITS
FROM THE SACRED INDIAN CITY OF VARANASI

City Lion Press, 2018

THESE INTIMATE PORTRAITS from the alleys close to the Ganges River were taken in winter when the river mist rose into the alleys, often persisting throughout the day. These alleys are among the oldest continuously inhabited places on the planet.

Varanasi is known as the City of Learning and Burning, referring both to the city's numerous schools, universities, ashrams, and pundits, as well as the many funeral pyres where faithful Hindus burn their dead by the river. Life and death are often juxtaposed in this chaotic and ancient city.

While the photographs portray people from all walks of life—and from differing faiths, ages, and social standing—they are mostly of people that others tend to consider outcasts and shy away from: the poor, street-dwellers, beggars, rickshaw pullers, widows discarded by their families, mourners with their shaved heads.

Printed in Great Britain
by Amazon

81478460R00087